Platonic Production

Other works of Stanley Rosen from St. Augustine's Press

The Ancients and the Moderns
Rethinking Modernity

Essays in Philosophy:
Ancient

Essays in Philosophy
Modern

G.W.F. Hegel
An Introduction to the Science of Wisdom

The Limits of Analysis

Metaphysics in Ordinary Language

Nihilism
A Philosophical Essay

Plato's Sophist
The Drama of Original and Image

Plato's Statesman
The Web of Politics

Plato's Symposium

The Question of Being
A Reversal of Heidegger

Also

Logos and Eros
Essays Honoring Stanley Rosen
Edited by Nalin Ranasinghe

Platonic Production
Theme and Variations

The Gilson Lectures

Stanley Rosen

Edited with an introduction by Andy German

ST. AUGUSTINE'S PRESS
South Bend, Indiana

Manufactured in the United States of America

1 2 3 4 5 6   19 18 17 16 15 14

Library of Congress Cataloging in Publication Data
Rosen, Stanley, 1929–
[Production platonicienne. English]
Platonic production: theme and variations: the Gilson lectures / Stanley Rosen; edited with an introduction by Andy German.
pages cm
Includes bibliographical references and index.
ISBN 978-1-58731-642-5 (hardback)
1. Plato. 2. Heidegger, Martin, 1889–1976. I. Title.
B395.R74513 2013
184 – dc23   2013026616

ST. AUGUSTINE'S PRESS
www.staugustine.net

Contents

ACKNOWLEDGMENTS

Collaboration on philosophical work with one's former teacher is a happy coincidence of duty and pleasure. In the present case, however, both the sense of a duty to complete this work and the pleasure in bringing it to the reading public have been made keener by loss. A few days before this volume went to press, Prof. Stanley Rosen died. Those who were his students had the great good fortune of watching someone exert every fiber of his being in living out Aristotle's statement: "καὶ ἔστι τοῦ φιλοσόφου περὶ πάντων δύνασθαι θεωρεῖν– "And it belongs to the philosopher to be capable of contemplating all things."

My warmest thanks to Bruce Fingerhut, Benjamin Fingerhut, and St. Augustine's Press for their initiative in bringing these lectures to publication in English and the attention, patience, and help they have gladly proffered along the way.

Nothing would be possible without my wife Chana, who has believed, hoped and endured all things.

EDITOR'S PREFACE

This volume contains an English version of the Etienne Gilson Lectures, delivered by Professor Stanley Rosen at the Institut Catholique-Paris in 2003. A French edition appeared as *La production platonicienne: Thème et Variations* (Paris: P.U.F, 2005).

These are *lectures*, not a systematic interpretative work on Heidegger or Plato. They are an attempt to think aloud and "on one's feet," as it were, about some of the deepest metaphysical questions which are raised by reading these two thinkers. In preparing the manuscript for English publication with St. Augustine's Press, I was guided by the desire to preserve, as far as possible, the manner in which the lectures were delivered. Accordingly, the conversational tone of Prof. Rosen's remarks was maintained throughout and I have refrained from burdening his text with a full apparatus of scholarly notes beyond those which he placed in the original manuscript in order to mention them during his talks. My own editorial notes are limited to clarifications, the provision of fuller citations or translations of particularly important passages on which Rosen remarks, or to pointing out interesting links to treatments in his other works.

The same general sensibility governs the introductory essay. It aims to enter into the "movement of thinking" exhibited in the lectures and follow it a bit further into the *Auseinandersetzung* between Heidegger and Plato. I make no pretense to a full engagement with all of the themes and controversies in the vast scholarly literature on both thinkers and their relationship. This is not to say that I have not been mindful of that literature or excellently well nourished by it. A bibliographical sample (by no means complete) of some of the works which were consulted in the lectures and the introductory essay, and which treat the issues raised there, can be found at the end of the volume.

INTRODUCTORY ESSAY
Discovery, Production, and Time:
The Problem of the 'Horizon' of Philosophy in Plato and Heidegger

Stanley Rosen has been having it out with Heidegger for the better part of fifty years. At the heart of their long debate and at the heart of the lectures presented here is Plato, and Heidegger's assessment of Plato's place in Western philosophical history. One might wonder why this should still be the case, especially after so much work has been done (not least by Rosen himself) to challenge Heidegger's interpretation of the dialogues.[1] What, in other words, is still at stake in grappling with Heidegger's Plato?

It is clear straightaway that the stakes are not simply philological, despite the great philological concentration which characterizes Heidegger's readings of Greek philosophy and Rosen's critique of them. Perhaps a better approach is to see their disagreement as resembling a medieval disputation in the best sense of

---

1   Even Heidegger himself later admitted the "untenable" nature of his interpretation of the relationship of truth to correctness (*orthotês*), a crucial point in his treatment of the Cave allegory. See *EP,* 87. In a conversation with one of his students, Georg Picht, Heidegger confessed that the "structure of Platonic thought is totally obscure to me." Quoted in Catalin Partenie and Tom Rockmore, *Heidegger and Plato: Toward Dialogue* (Evanston, Ill: Northwestern University Press, 2005), xxiv.

what this might have been but never really was – an argument about a text that was in fact an argument *through* the text, toward a more comprehensive and shared concern. In the ideal case (where the disputation was not just another skirmish in the battle for *propaganda fide*), the disagreement between the medieval priest and rabbi about the correct interpretation of Scripture would be in the service of what they agreed upon – the ultimate importance of knowing the will of God.[2] Summarily stated, Rosen disagrees with Heidegger because he agrees with him on the pre-eminent philosophical importance of the question: "Is philosophical knowledge best characterized as discovery or as production?"[3]

For Heidegger, however, this question (like all other decisive questions in our tradition) presupposes a basic relation to the world, a metaphysical horizon, within which it is first possible to raise it. This horizon was first articulated, for the Western tradition, by Plato. Only now, standing in the "rubble" of that tradition, are we in a position to reflect upon it completely, and thus, give thought a new direction.[4]

It is with this assessment of Western metaphysics as "Platonism" that Rosen disagrees, occasionally with some heat. But even this disagreement should not blind us to another crucial area of agreement. For both Rosen and Heidegger, Platonic thought is never the long-transcended beginning of Western spiritual history. The proper study of Plato always leads to the question of the coherence and prospects of the *contemporary* philosophical moment.[5]

---

2   A truly philosophical *disputatio* – *der Streit zwischen Denkern* – is what Heidegger calls "a lovers' quarrel about the matter itself" (*der Sache selbst*). *HB*, 167/256.

3   See p. 110. All references to the Gilson Lectures which follow shall appear parenthetically in the text.

4   There are numerous examples of this scattered throughout Heidegger's corpus. See *WdW*, 17/12. Cf. *EM*, 139/191: "Plato is the fulfillment (*Vollendung*) of the beginning."

5   See *PLW*, 234–235/181–182: "Plato's doctrine of 'truth' is therefore not

The task of this essay, then, is a dual one: first, to unfold the central themes of Prof. Rosen's lectures, elucidating, as far as possible, the matter at issue between him and Heidegger *and* between Heidegger and Plato. Subsequently, we will turn to some reflections on a "Platonic" problem that arises from Heidegger's assessment of modern nihilism. This will serve, I hope, as an example of how to think through the questions which animate these lectures and Prof. Rosen's work more generally.

The lectures begin from Heidegger's insistence that Aristotle is a "more radical and scientific Plato" (11) and hence the "more correct path of access" to Platonic thought. Rosen aims to show that this is a faulty assumption. Platonic Ideas cannot be simply assimilated into the Aristotelian doctrine of being, not to mention the fact that there is an ambiguity within that doctrine itself.

The Aristotelian corpus has two treatments of *ousia*. In the *Categories*, the categorical determinations possessed by any composite, separate substance (any *sunolon*), such as Socrates or a horse, are analyzed into a subject and all its predicates. But in Book Zeta of the *Metaphysics*, the dominant sense of *ousia* is *eidos*, the essential form of the individual, grasped, not by categorical predication, but all at once in intuition. Since both senses are referred to as *ousiai*, Heidegger can argue that in Aristotle logos is already detached from its primordial sense as the logos *of* Being and is turning instead into a predicative, discursive tool of a subject which stands over against Being.[6]

Neither here nor elsewhere does Rosen deny that there is an element of truth in Heidegger's diagnosis of philosophy as a decline from thinking about the whole into formal logic and philosophy of language, or from "substance to syntax" (4). But if so, he argues, Western thought is decayed *Aristotelianism*, not Platonism. Plato provides no analysis of the internal structure of

something that is past. It is historically 'present'" . . . It is "still in place" as "the ever–advancing world history of the planet. . . ."

6   Or as he puts it elsewhere, a "tribunal" (*Gerichtshof*) that presides over Being. *EM*, 188/191.

the Idea.[7] We see the Idea in noetic apprehension, which is then rendered only partly accessible to discursive intelligence. Nor does Plato try to articulate anything like what Heidegger calls a *Durchschnittsbegriff*, an average or general concept of being.[8] He is not, then, a less technically competent Aristotle or a rough first draft of ontology, but is trying to do something else. There is even a sense in which the presentation of human life in the dialogues is motivated by concerns very close to those of Heidegger's *Daseinanalytik*. In Plato, however, the analysis is not of existential categories but of the variety of human types and their interactions (10).[9]

It is no doubt an oversimplification, though a serviceable one for all that, to see Socrates as the unity underlying the kaleidoscopic variety of types of existence. By this I mean that the portrayal of Socrates – who laughs gently but never weeps, who can go whole days and nights without eating or sleeping or even moving, who practices the fine art of dying and being dead – is not hagiography; it isn't even biography. Plato's Socrates is a human parallel to the *kallipolis* in the *Republic:* a "pattern laid up in heaven," which unifies the restless motion of living, questioning intelligence and the eternal, "satisfied" immobility of the Forms. The different kinds of possible life depicted in the dialogues – the hedonists, money-makers, warriors, rulers, poets – are different possible refractions of desire. The Socratic "paradigm" interprets the total significance of those refractions – what they all point to, however incompletely.

---

7   Arguably, according to Rosen, Aristotle does not provide this either. For a fuller treatment see his *The Question of Being: A Reversal of Heidegger* (South Bend, Ind: St. Augustine's Press, 2002), 26–35.

8   In Aristotle's terms: *to on* is *katholou malista pantôn. Met.,* 1001a21, and cf. *GPP*, 30/22.

9   Hence the irreducible importance of attention to the dramatic details of all Platonic dialogues in Rosen's lifelong project of interpretation. This holds true even for the later dialogues, where the dramatic landscape is ostensibly sparse. See Stanley Rosen, *Plato's Symposium*, 2nd Ed. (New Haven: Yale University Press, 1987) and *Plato's Sophist: The Drama of Original and Image* (New Haven: Yale University Press, 1983) for examples of Rosen's treatment of dialogues on opposite ends of the dramatic continuum.

Lectures II and III address the two main (and not always mutually compatible) strands in Heidegger's "Platonism": Being as eternal presence (*Anwesenheit*, or *parousia*), on the one hand, or Being understood in analogy to something produced (*hergestellt*) by the workings of the human spirit (and thus ultimately by the will to power), on the other. For Heidegger, either restriction of the question of Being (to "present-at-hand" intelligibility or to utility) seals the fate of metaphysics.[10]

The *locus classicus* of Heidegger's treatment of the ideas as "produced" is his analysis, in the *Nietzsche* lectures, of the passage in Book X of the *Republic* where Socrates refers to an "idea" of a bed.[11] Rosen's main criticism is that Heidegger takes no notice of the political context in which Socrates makes this frankly unprecedented suggestion. The idea of the Bed is broached as part of a radical depreciation of poetry, which is placed on a level below not only philosophy, but even mere craftsmanship, as part of the effort to preserve the unity of the perfect city from the disintegrative power of poetic imagination (28–29). That radical depreciation is itself ambiguous in Plato, but this means that the "artifactual" understanding of the Idea discussed there cannot be taken as Plato's teaching in any straightforward manner.

Heidegger also fails to note a second, most important fact about Socrates' presentation. Though the god is said to make (*poiêin*) or produce (*apergazesthai*) the "bed that is by nature" (the *en tê phusei ousa klinê*), there is also a preponderance of mentions of "begetting" or "growing" (*phuteuein*) the Idea of the bed. The divine being in this passage is a *phutourgos*, a divine gardener, not a *dêmiourgos* (craftsman). If anything, Socrates distinguishes between natural beings (*phusei onta*) and craftsmanship,

---

10 The capitalized form "Being" is restricted to Heidegger's specific sense of the term *Sein*. When discussing *ousia* or *to on* in Plato and Aristotle, or being as a philosophical problem more generally, I will use the lower case.

11 *R.* 596a10fff. For a discussion of the origin of the concepts of *actualitas* and *essentia* in the "productive behavior of Dasein" in Greek ontology, see *GPP*, 140–159/100–112, (specifically, 147–148/105–106).

rather than identifying them.[12] He also qualifies his usual emphasis on instantaneous, noetic vision of the Ideas (27 and 41) in a way that brings him *closer* to Heidegger (30). What the carpenter sees in making a wooden bed is not a static picture of a perfect bed, but its *dunamis* or function, and hence also the complex of natural relations and capacities to which it is suited (a surface for reclining, necessitated by the finite endurance of our body and its need for rest, etc.). What neither we nor the god create is *phusis*, that complex of relations and capacities which dictates our need for beds. At this altogether more fundamental level, there is no doctrine of "production" in Plato.

The third lecture turns to the identification of true being with what is eternally self-same and present, or *ontôs on* with *aei on*. As Rosen puts it:

> . . . . Plato takes his bearings by that which is presented, where he himself [Heidegger] refers primarily to the horizon of presentation. . . . Platonism both overlooks the temporality of presence and obscures the fundamental process of opening and lighting-up that is the necessary condition for the visibility of any present entity. (44)[13]

The Platonic preference for presence and for metaphors of light and visibility is a first step toward reifying Being, controlling it, putting it to work. Metaphysics is thus "humanized" in Plato, a distant ancestor of both modern subjectivity and technology.[14]

At no point is Rosen aiming for a simple refutation of this point. He persistently highlights the common ground shared by Plato and Heidegger but obscured by the latter (47–49). The Platonic preference for visual metaphors in describing the Ideas

---

12 The latter term is reserved for the carpenter and the painter. See specifically R. 597c4–5 and d3–5.
13 WMF, 62/43: "The Greeks understood *Seiendheit* in the sense of enduring presence" (*beständiger Anwesenheit*).
14 SZ, 24–25/46–47, and cf. HB, 312/240 and AWP, 131.

does not change the fact that their presence to the "eye of the soul" is incomplete. As Plato indicates in numerous ways, there is never a complete grasp of the Ideas. For one thing, the human intellect is unthinkable without soul and life, and hence it is part of genesis, not eternity.[15] While everyday experience would be impossible without intelligible "presence," Plato remains aware of the penumbra of absence or darkness that surrounds and qualifies our apprehension of the Idea (49). Truth must be wrested from this darkness by a cognition which itself is partly a dweller in the realm of shadows.

Now, this debate about truth, presence and absence can easily descend into truism. What serious thinker, after all (to say nothing of any ordinarily reflective and intelligent person), has not noticed the finitude of our cognitive powers, or the prevalence of ignorance, error, and obscurity from which we wring out whatever truth we can only by the greatest exertion? The task of philosophy is not simply to restate the obvious, but to give the most precise possible articulation of how truth and falsehood (or "presence and absence") are interwoven. This Plato does by supplementing formal structure with eros, the psychic *dunamis* which is naturally directed toward knowledge, and is not at all "present-at-hand" or "ready-to-hand." It is in fact formless, and sometimes, dangerous. Platonism, then, cannot be simply equivalent to the hypothesis of Ideas (54–55).

Close examination of the philosophical significance of eros has, of course, been a principal emphasis in Rosen's own work,[16] and in these lectures he notes that ". . . eros does not play an important role in Heidegger's discussions of Plato, although there is a kind of surrogate for eros in Heidegger's own concept of *Sorge* (care). . . ." (57). Though this is true of Heidegger's 1940 essay, *Platons Lehre von der Wahrheit*, it would be unfair to say that he

---

15   *Ti.* 30b1–5 and see Rosen's discussion of the *Phaedrus* on p. 59 below.
16   One could easily multiply examples so far as to list Rosen's entire *oeuvre*. As a representative sample, I would direct the reader to "The Quarrel between Philosophy and Poetry" (New York: Routledge, 1988) and also *Plato's Symposium*, 2nd ed. (New Haven: Yale University Press, 1987).

misses eros completely. There is a remarkable treatment of it in his 1931–1932 lecture course (*Vom Wesen der Wahrheit: zu Platons Höhlengleichnis und Theätet*) which bears remarking upon here.

Curiously enough, although *Vom Wesen der Wahrheit* has become famous for its invocations of Plato's role in the decline of Western *Seinsgeschichte*, Heidegger displays a greater affinity with Plato in those lectures than perhaps anywhere else. Not only is there an extended meditation on eros, but Heidegger refrains from simply identifying Platonism with the Ideas. He notes that *eidos* is something that always "remains a question" for Plato, never a calcified "theory."[17] It is here, where the two seem closest, however, that we can get a firm grip on their differences.

Heidegger identifies Platonic *eros* with Dasein's primordial striving for Being, a striving which is presupposed by any act of sense-perception, because any such act is not an act *of* the eye, ear, or nose, but of the soul, as a unity of a particular kind (a *mia tis idea* in the language of *Theaetetus* 184d). It is nonsensical to say that the eye or nose perceives. An ensouled being perceives by *making use of* (or "through") eyes and ears. But this is so only because the soul is always already reaching out, beyond particular perceptions, to what all of them have in common, towards the Being of what is perceived. By its very reaching out toward Being, the soul constitutes, or, as Heidegger puts it, "upholds" (*WdW*, 232/166) a "region of perceivability" within which anything perceivable is available to us. Eros is this "striving for Being," or *Seinserstrebnis*.[18]

At this point, Heidegger invokes the distinction, familiar from *Being and Time*, between authenticity (*Eigentlichkeit*) and inauthenticity (*Uneigentlichkeit*). There are *eigentlich* and *uneigentlich* ways in which to strive for something and eros is the most "authentic striving" and simultaneously the most "authentic having," because unlike the inauthentic forms, it does not aim to

17 *WdW*, 172–173/125.
18 *WdW*, 216/155. Cf. *Nietzsche*, I, 226/194: "Only to the extent that Being is able to elicit 'erotic' power in its relation to man, is man capable of thinking about Being and overcoming oblivion of Being."

assimilate the object into itself or vice versa. The erotic striving keeps the object "as striven for . . . so that the striver finds himself from that for which he strives" and thus returns to himself:

> . . . he who thus strives is held fast in his own self by the object of his striving, such that this striving provides the measure and law [*Maß und Gesetz*] for his comportment to beings, enabling existence from the ground of beings as a whole. Thereby, however, i.e., in authentic striving, man *holds himself* as an existing being in the midst of beings . . . (*WdW*, 215–216/154–155)

Eros then, is not mere "chasing after." Nor is it an impulse which propels outward because of some interior lack which must be filled. It is a kind of reflective self-constitution, a "seeing" striving (*sehendes Streben*)(*WdW*, 223/159) in which Dasein itself is sustained, or "carried" (*WdW*, 216/155).

Much of this description is of course very close to the dialogues. The souls of Socrates' different interlocutors are distinguished by the kind and degree of comprehensiveness of their eros.[19] And to the degree that, for Plato, one cannot understand the psychic capacities, activities and choices that constitute a life without understanding how the soul is influenced by the objects *towards which* it is directed, it can be said that eros, like *Streben*, is *the* activity by means of which recognizably human life is constituted. Indeed, one of Rosen's main tasks in interpreting the cave allegory is to highlight the Heideggerian ambience of this paradigmatically Platonic text on just this point. I note a few details of that interpretation in order to fill out the discussion of Heideggerian and Platonic eros.

The cave allegory, Rosen argues, does *not* overlook "the fundamental experience" of *Verborgenheit* which is the ground of seeking after *Un-verborgenheit*. It is an allegorical presentation of

---

19   One thinks of the differences between Glaucon and Adeimantus in the *Republic*, or Charmides and Critias in the *Charmides*, but there are numerous other examples.

exactly that experience.[20] In the cave, cognition is shown to have a dimension which corresponds to Heideggerian concealment, "from which the truth must be grasped and brought into the light" (68). This aspect of the allegory is not given due weight in Heidegger's correlation of the interior of the cave with everyday existence and the surface of the earth with the "authentic being of beings."[21]

For Rosen, the interior of the cave represents not only pre-philosophical political life (the rule of *nomos*), or everyday existence, nor is it a realm left behind for good by the exit into the sunlight. It represents an altogether deeper and more hidden level of psychic life; a shadow-loving, pre-discursive, "sub-natural" element always present in the soul. Making sense of it requires understanding what Socrates means by restricting the prisoners to observing the shadows on the wall without seeing their originals:

> . . . the shadows within the cave are, for the prisoners, perceptually entirely distinct from their artifactual originals, which are not seen at all. . . . The viewing of shadows in the cave is thus the perception of copies of copies. It is nothing like the perception of objects, but more like mistaking one's reflection in a pool for an actual face. It is therefore misleading to identify the first stage . . . with some actual perceptual or cognitive state. The viewing of shadows is more like a basis-step in a procedure that retains the shadows at all higher levels. (71)

One might be tempted to identify the viewing of the shadows with the level of *eikasia*, or image-making, the lowest step in the divided line image. Strictly speaking, however, the situation of the prisoners must be even lower than *eikasia*, since they do not see the shadows on the wall as shadows *of* anything. Nor does it seem

20   *WdW*, 13/9.
21   See *PLW*, 211/164. This schema persists in the later lecture course as well. See *WdW*, 28/22.

that the prisoners at this stage can have the power of speech,[22] or, for that matter, any reflexive self-awareness, since they can see neither themselves nor other human beings in whose presence they could become aware of, and thus "return" to, themselves. The prisoners are wholly captive to the procession of shadows which pass in and out of view. They exist in a world which is unique: it is almost completely closed in upon itself, without even the degree of reflexivity or psychic unity necessary to ask the "What is it?" question about the images seen on the wall.

And then, suddenly, a prisoner is released from his bonds, without any explanation, internal to the dramatic context, of how this is possible. It simply happens "by nature" (*phusei*), which Rosen identifies with eros (76). On this interpretation, then, the allegory presents the "sub-natural" or "closed" soul together with the impulse outward, toward the originals of the shadows, but no genetic account of the move from one state to the other. The soul is always already both open and closed to the whole.[23]

There is a deep sense, then, in which Plato would agree that the soul is what Heidegger calls "primordially relationship-to . . ." (*Verhältnis zu*) and that "what it means for a human being to be . . . a *self*, can be understood only from this phenomenon of striving for Being" (*WdW,* 233/166). However, since this grasp or process is never completed – since, for example, even the released prisoner must eventually return to the cave – it is false to say that Plato has a doctrine of the complete *parousia* of intelligibility.

But if we bring together the Ideas, eros, and the shadow consciousness of the cave, how close do we come to the role which Heidegger assigns to *alêtheia,* concealment and temporality in thinking? In one sense we are very close, as already seen. But in another and more decisive sense, the fact that the soul or Dasein is related to, or open to being, leaves unanswered the question of how exactly "measure and law," or intelligible structure, are given

22   Note the conditional nature of Socrates' statement at *R.* 515b4.
23   See pp. 2 and 95 below.

to us within that relation. Let us look at Heidegger's further comments on the same passage from the *Theaetetus* (186a5–9) which we discussed earlier. When Theaetetus says that being (*ousia*) is what the soul examines "itself by itself," Socrates continues:

> And the similar too and the dissimilar, and "the same" and other?
>
> Yes.
>
> And what about this? Beautiful, ugly, good and bad?
>
> It's my opinion that it's the being of these things in their mutual relations which the soul most especially examines (*skopeisthai*), calculating (*analogizomenê*) in itself the past and present things in relation to the future (*pros ta mellonta*)."

In analyzing this passage, Heidegger asks what it means to say that the soul "examines" good, bad, beautiful and ugly. Is it possible for something to appear to us in one of these ways if Dasein had not already been *attuned* to goodness or beauty as such? And do not verbs such as *skopeisthai* and *analogizesthai* denote concernful, purposive dealing-with and calculation rather than disinterested, theoretical contemplation? And is it unimportant that the text mentions that this comportment toward "the being of things" is *pros ta mellonta*: in relation to, in respect of, in view of the future?

Plato, then, had "stumbled upon" the primacy of Dasein's constant projection of itself into the future in any ontological understanding of time (and hence of such things as good, bad, etc., which appear in Dasein's temporal existence): exactly the basis of Heidegger's analyses of "care," "state of mind" or "attunement" and "primordial temporality," in *Being and Time*. But Plato's insight quickly "disappears into the night of that blind logic of understanding . . ." (*WdW*, 226/162). Theaetetus, we note, does not say that the beautiful or good are themselves within time. Rather, a sounder interpretation of passage is that the erotic, temporally-bound soul calculates about them in relation to *its* future (not *their* future). As I will argue later, the crux of the disagreement between Plato and Heidegger turns on what we make of this difference.

The Cave allegory serves as a pivot to the fifth and sixth lectures, which focus on two main questions:

1. To what extent is nature in Plato benevolently predisposed toward human flourishing?

2. If indeed the question "discovery or production?" is decisive, can we make defensible Plato's insight that nature as *eidos* is "outside" the process of mentation – and thus discovered, not produced?

The link between these two questions is Heidegger's claim that Plato's Idea of the Good has a utilitarian tincture. It is that which "empowers" or makes the Ideas (and hence beings) suitable (*tauglich*) for human use, thus constituting a further example of the "humanization" of metaphysics and the restriction of the *Seinsfrage* (*WdW,* 106/77).[24]

Rosen sees no need to deny that the Ideas are useful to us. Utility is a proper part of what it means to be an *on agathon,* and one of the most immediate ways we experience "goodness." However, this does not entail that it encompasses the entirety of what Plato intends by the Good. In fact, there is no direct Platonic route from the undeniable fact that we are natural beings to the claim that we can live in accord with a "given" natural perfection ultimately tied to the Good as an ontological principle. Whatever Plato's ultimate teaching regarding the Good, its writ does not extend into human life in an uncomplicated manner, as evidenced by the fact that a healthy political order, if achievable at all, requires the vigorous application of force and noble lies. Mankind is sick, not political, by nature (94). We try to construct a healthy political and psychic order in the imperfect light which the natural order provides us.

---

24 Cf. *N,* I, 198/165–166. (The German pagination here refers to *GA,* 6.2.)

But Plato also persistently emphasizes the peculiar fact that nature grounds the effort to live *kata phusin* (95) and also unravels us at the same time. In the myth of the reversed cosmos in the *Statesman* there is no eros, and most probably no philosophy, during the "golden age," or benevolent cosmic cycle which is directly under the governance of Cronus. Eros and philosophy are residents of the present cycle, in which the god withdraws and allows the cosmos to run on its own finite quantity of "prudence." This same cycle, in which human flourishing and perfection are possible, is also the one in which the cosmos is slowly but inexorably disintegrating toward the "ancient disharmony" with which it is periodically afflicted. This myth is the most striking example of the problem, though hardly the only one.[25]

Consequently, Platonic *phusis* has at least two conflicting senses: it is the natural standards of completeness and perfection but also the various ways in which we can deviate, or fall away from, those same standards; these, too, after all, are "natural." On this point at least, there is a marked affinity between Plato and those modern thinkers (such as Rousseau and Kant to name only two) for whom man is only partly at home within nature. For this reason, we might have more to learn from Plato in late modernity, than from Aristotle (109).[26]

But even if Plato is more modern than Aristotle, it would seem he leaves us with one incontestably and indigestibly "ancient" bone lodged in the throat – namely, the Ideas. Consequently, throughout his many books and essays, Rosen does not shy away from confronting head-on the task of trying to defend Plato's identification of "that which is" with *eidos*. This is the goal of the

---

25 *Pol.* 269a1ff, and cf. specifically 273c6–d1 on the "*tês palaias anarmostias pathos.*" In a sense, the whole of the *Timaeus* is a meditation on this problem. For Rosen's fullest treatment of the ambiguous nature of nature in Plato, see his *Plato's Statesman: The Web of Politics* (South Bend, Indiana: St. Augustine's Press, 2004).

26 Heidegger himself noted that Aristotle was more "Greek" than his illustrious teacher. Cf. *Nietzsche II*, 409–10. This section of the Nietzsche lectures does not appear in Farrell-Krell's English version.

sixth and final lecture: not to give a "canonical statement" of the doctrine of Ideas (which Plato himself never does) but to "indicate the intellectual work that these texts demand of us in the attempt to determine the truth" (113). As I understand it, this work has two parts: first to refocus our attention on the ordinary experience which necessitates positing something like the Ideas; second, to see if the Ideas provide what Socrates calls the "safest" explanation of how such experience is possible in the first place.[27]

In the *Phaedo,* Socrates gives an "autobiographical" account of his youthful turn from the "inquiry into nature" (*peri phuseôs historian*) to his own "method jumbled together at random" (*Phd.* 97b6–7). The crucial phenomenon which leads Socrates to become "wonderfully keen" on the knowledge of nature is the fact of coming-to-be and passing away. As examples of the things which piqued his curiosity, he mentions physical growth, the conditions for the possibility of cognition, the causes of memory and sensation. Interestingly, he does not mention logical or formal entities or the status of goodness or justice. It is rather the immediate experience of change, of "what happens to things in the sky and on earth" (*Phd.* 96b9–c1), which lead him to ask about cause (*aitia*).

But there is no experience at all of "change" as such. We experience only identifiable things undergoing change – i.e., things at once determinate and yet able to take on new determinations (of quality, relation, location, etc). In order to explain this change, then, the causes must be somehow separate from the *explanandum* and thus from the transformation it undergoes. If the causes, too, were in flux we would be forced into a further search for the principles underlying *their* transformation. Finally, the causes must account for the determinacy of items of genesis, since Socrates is looking for "the cause of each thing, why it comes to be, why it perishes and why it *is*" (*dia ti esti*) (*Phd.* 96a10).

From this, Rosen deduces three "central axioms of Platonism" (113), around which the dialogues, for all their diversity, continually revolve:

27 *Phd.* 100e1.

(I) *Determinacy* (115) – To be is to be something identifiable.

(II) *Separation* (115–116) – the Idea, qua *aitia*, must be separate from the changes undergone by the entity of which it is the *aitia*.

(III) *Knowledge* (118–119) – knowledge of the particulars of genesis is not possible. Knowledge in the strict sense is of the *eidos*.[28]

Rosen staunchly defends the first axiom but rejects the second (120) and hence the third (or accepts them only in a very qualified sense). Like Aristotle, Rosen too argues that it cannot be that we identify the particular cow before us by "looking off" to a perfect, separate, Idea of the Cow somewhere else, of which the cow in the manger is but a faded and slightly mangled photocopy. This leads directly to Rosen's criticisms of the third axiom, the point at which he seems to diverge sharply from the "orthodox" statement of Platonism.

If it is true that *epistêmê* is not of the particular but of the Idea, then knowledge is actually quite thin gruel (119). The Idea provides only the ontological properties (such as sameness, difference, etc.) present in every intelligible structure, as well as the "uncuttable" unity (117) of those properties which make the cow in the manger what it is. The Idea is not, however, a complex, nonsensible structure of the "real" predicates of the cow. If the Idea of the Cow contained *all* of the real predicates of cow-hood, we could milk it.

Rather, what happens is that when we study an individual horse or cow, we see it as a determinate unity, the same as itself and different from every other thing, thanks to the Idea. But what this (the cow) is, as opposed specifically to that (the horse), we do not learn from some separate Idea of the Cow, but from studying the individual, empirical instance, since the empirical instances, *of which* there are Ideas, have the properties which identify them as

---

28 *Republic*, 477a3: ". . . *to men pantelôs on pantelôs gnôston*. . ." ("What is entirely, is entirely knowable").

"this thing here." The Idea, by contrast, does not allow an inspection, analysis, or dissection into parts:

> For how can we derive the eidetic properties of what it is to be a cow from the empirical properties such as "four footed," "chews a cud," "yields milk," and so on? The answer is that we cannot, because *there are no purely eidetic properties of what it is to be a cow*. There are instead empirical properties that are subject to change. What does not change is the fact that we can perceive and study the empirical cow because of its adherence to the ontological properties of the structure of intelligibility that Plato regularly speaks of as "Ideas." It is this structure that regulates change and makes changing things intelligible. (128)

What, then, is the proper ratio of production to discovery in knowing the cow?

> . . . we produce, or share in the production of, a good many things, including the instances of perceptual experience. We also produce the calculative reasoning by which the formal properties of experience are rendered more fully intelligible. But we cannot produce the formal properties themselves. For example, our neurophysiology, together with the laws of optics, produce the sensory individual known in everyday life as a cow. But it does not produce the fact that to be is to be something of such-and-such a kind. (129–130)

What it means to be a cow, then, may change (128). The radical implication is that as empirical cows change, so too would the elements of the kind, or Idea, "Cow." What does not change is that the ontological structure of intelligibility *must* manifest itself in unified and determinate particulars, whatever their internal structure (ibid). This is Rosen's resolution of what Heidegger had always identified as the fundamental problem, the relationship of Being to Time: Being is a-temporal intelligibility that must manifest, or "give of" itself *in time* as this or that determinate, temporally bound, entity. But this means that determinacy, or the ontic, is the intelligible "face" or "look" *of* Being, not the occlusion of a yet more primordial process. Or rather, there never was, nor could be any other access to Being than through its intelligible face, the determinate beings. *Contra* Heidegger, there was never a "fall" from some more original experience of *Sein*.

In reflecting on all of this, one should keep in mind another insight common to Heidegger and Rosen; namely, that genuinely philosophical problems are not puzzles waiting to be "solved." Their speculative value derives precisely from the fact that they are enigmas which continually point to, rather than occlude, the enigmatic character of Being (111). In that spirit, we can raise two questions here.

If the empirical properties which particularize the Ideas are subject to change, while the ontological constituents of intelligibility are not, why indeed would there *not* be Ideas of artifacts? After all, the cellular phone too, must be identical to itself and different from the lamp, a unity of certain properties without which I could not identify it. As Rosen points out however (35), to assert the existence of ideas of artifacts would reverse the relation between possibility and actuality. The number of Ideas, and the *kosmos noêtos*, would depend for its completeness upon the limitless potential of human ingenuity, collapsing the distinction between *theoria* and *poiêsis*.

There is another thought-provoking difficulty, which Rosen himself notes at many different points in his lectures. While accepting the "relevance of Platonic Ideas of logical entities and structures," he is "extremely dubious about the extension of the doctrine to other kinds of beings, such as cows and horses, not to mention justice and beauty . . ." (120). It is not even clear what it would mean for there to be an "Idea" of a just or beautiful human act, since human actions are inherently circumstantial, contextual, contingent. And what is more, Plato never explains how "looking off" at any Idea would make prudent action possible (84). In what way is it true, then, that the hypothesis of Ideas answers Socrates' problem in the *Phaedo,* of how to find the *aitia* which grounds our ability to judge the better or worse, or the just and the beautiful and their opposites?[29]

Rosen's answer is that it does so only in an indirect sense, via the philosophical eros to know the good. As he writes, "The Good makes existence and cognition possible, but it does not tell us what to do, and certainly not what is morally or politically good and what is evil." The philosopher will be an excellent demiurge of "temperance, justice, and the vulgar virtues altogether" (VI. 500d6–9), but this is only because "for Plato, an action is finally good or evil depending upon whether it is compatible or not with philosophy."[30]

In short, as the Sun image teaches, the Good is the source of the light, or intelligibility, which makes visible the determinate beings of experience. Our desire, the source of our actions, is, when understood completely, always directed toward the Good, which is "what every soul pursues." Justice, to take one example, is not an Idea; our judging things as just or unjust is entirely derivative of the way we measure and adjust our desires in light of the intelligible whole illuminated by the Good and only the philosopher does this in the fullest sense. Philosophical eros is thus the mediating term between the source of intelligibility and the life we must construct in its light.

The Good, however, is neither self-conscious nor historical. According to the sun image, it does not account for the origin of the soul, but only for the being and intelligibility of the "things known." The consequence is that as the philosopher tries to follow up on, and articulate, the divinations we have about the goodness of intelligibility he or she is being led away from everyday life

---

29 *Phd.* 99a2–3. Socrates would have been off to Megara or Boeotia, had he not thought it more "just and beautiful" to remain in prison.

30 See p. 85 below. Cf. with Chapter 4 of Rosen's *Nihilism: A Philosophical Essay* (New Haven: Yale University Press, 1969), especially, 163–185.

and its concerns. Justice, prudence or moderation are, as the *Republic* notes in the passage quoted above, demiurgic *productions* of philosophy. At best they are ministerial to philosophy, but for the most part, the philosopher wants as little as possible to do with the *tôn anthrôpôn pragmata* (this, of course, does not mean that he can get what he wants). Praxis is either assimilated into theory or its status is radically demoted.

But does this not mean that even after we have jettisoned the disjunction between the visible and noetic *topoi*, a version of the *chorismos* problem returns through the back door? The chasm has simply been internalized into the soul, as the disjunction between its theoretical and practical capacities. Rosen writes elsewhere that the significance of Plato's Idea of the Good as the ground for intelligibility and for intelligence is to "unite life and formal structure," but it seems that the net effect of the Good on human life is to pull man in two different directions, not unite him.[31]

The interesting question that now arises is whether we could resolve the difficulty in a radical way, by ridding ourselves altogether of Plato's link between reason, separate Ideas, and a non-historical and non-subjective horizon of thinking (the Good). It is obviously out of the question to tackle such an issue in full in this context. However, I do think it possible to show, in some detail, how a representative Heideggerian theme – the ascendancy of technological civilization – ultimately corroborates Rosen's assertion that Platonism is not a doctrine at all, but a problem.[32]

* * * * * * * *

Heidegger, unlike many others, does not engage in (ultimately impotent) protests against technology, whether in general or with regard to the question of its specific applications or consequences. For him, such questions are, in any case, either tendentious or

---

31 *Nihilism*, 176.
32 Though I limit myself here largely to his essay, *Die Frage nach der Technik* and related texts, the themes developed there are emblematic of Heidegger's later work as a whole.

completely abstract until we have tunneled underneath them and asked what it means for something to be technological at all, or "What is the essence of technology?"

This essence cannot simply be a sum total of implements of varying complexity, nor is it a particular mode of manufacture. The essence of technology is not technological at all in the ordinary sense. Technology is a way that truth *happens*, a particular mode of *alêtheuein*, or the opening up and revealing of beings. Stated alternatively, it is a way in which Dasein causes beings to reveal some – but only some – aspects of their nature.[33]

Technology "reveals" by issuing a kind of challenge or provocation (*Herausforderung*) to nature. Man demands that nature provide itself to him as a supply of undifferentiated energy, or raw material, ready for use (*FNT*, 15–16/14). Technology does not make do with trusting itself to the keeping of natural forces; it sets upon them to release, store and thereby manipulate the transformative energy of those forces.[34] Thus, it is not simply a quantitatively massive improvement in instrumental power when compared, say, to Greek *technê*. It is a completely new way to categorize what things there really are and what they are there for. Beings as a whole are no longer articulated into a heterogeneity of essential kinds (or at least not only or principally that). Natural kinds are epiphenomena of undifferentiated mass-points moving in fields of force because for technological consciousness, nature is *Bestand*, a "standing-reserve" of pure, indeterminate energy awaiting disposition by human beings.

Heidegger therefore argues that the common conception of technology as the practical offspring of theoretical science has things exactly backward. The theoretical science which sets up,

---

33 *FNT*, 14/13 and cf. *HB*, 322/247: "It could even be that nature, in the face it turns toward the human being's technical mastery, is simply concealing its essence."

34 See *FNT*, 16/15 for Heidegger's explanation of the difference between technology and pre-modern manifestations of agriculture, tool use, modification of the lived environment, etc.

posits, or "frames" (*stellt*) nature as a quantifiable ratio of forces, is a research project which emerges from the technological impetus. Technology is entirely more fundamental, more primordial, than mathematical physics.[35] It is the last stop on the long metaphysical road opened by Plato, a consequence of an interpretation of the whole under a certain conception of human being in the cosmos,[36] and ultimately under the aspect of will to power. Viewed from such a perspective, it is inevitable that the earth can "show itself only as the object of an assault."[37]

The end result of technology would appear to be a world remade entirely in man's image. "It seems," Heidegger writes, "as though man everywhere and always encounters only himself" (*FNT*, 28/27). And yet this is a mirage. Man is rather in danger of interpreting himself as *Bestand*, as a "human resource," or more appropriately, *Stoff*.[38] In remaking the world in the image of technology, man encounters his true essence nowhere; he erases it (ibid).

To this point, elements of Heidegger's analysis should be familiar as a deepening of themes already found in reflection on the new sciences from Rousseau and Kant onward. In this tradition, the new scientific understanding of the world – with its demolition of teleology, its explanatory reductionism, its universal laws neutral to species difference – renders the distinct nature of human existence invisible. The uniquely Heideggerian element, however, is his denial that the "essence of technology" is a prod-

---

35 This does not entail chronological priority, as Heidegger well knew (*FNT* 22–23/21–22) and cf. *AWP*,116.

36 *HB*, 319/245. Cf. *HHA*, 91: "The essential origin of modern technology lies in the Platonic beginning of metaphysics."

37 *NW*, 100. And on the relation of this "assault" to the modern concept of the representing subject which must "create itself" as an absolutely certain metaphysical foundation, see *AWP*, 148–149.

38 *FNT*, 18/18. And cf. *AWP*, 152–153: "In the planetary imperialism of technologically organized man, the subjectivism of man attains its acme, from which point it will descend to the level of organized uniformity. . . . The modern freedom of subjectivity vanishes totally in the objectivity commensurate with it."

uct of human volition. Technology is "no mere handiwork (*Gemächte*) of man" (*FNT*, 19–20/18–19). Just as in *Being and Time*, the "fall" of Dasein into inauthenticity is not something which Dasein does, but a way it must necessarily *be*, so our challenge to nature, "framing" it within a technological conceptual framework, is an epiphenomenon of something which is *happening* to us.[39] Man, who challenges, orders and frames nature does so as challenged, set upon, even "framed" by Being itself. It is Being which, in the present epoch, "challenges" us to reveal beings technologically. Only within such an all-encompassing challenge can technological implements be what they are. This challenge is the "essence" of technology, which Heidegger names the *Ge-stell* or "En-framing."[40]

Therefore, any anthropocentric interpretation of technology is wrong from the ground up. Technology is a mode of *Being*'s revelation and Dasein, as Heidegger regularly insists, neither masters nor creates Being. The opposite is the case. Dasein is the place, or "clearing" within which Being must reveal itself in different ways during different historical eras. As the emergence-process from which all beings come forth to constitute a world, Being comes to presence and articulation only for a being that can speak and for whom something can appear as this or that, can have significance as this or that. This being is Dasein. What we call human nature is thus not a stable essence, such as "rational animal," but the *topos* of Being's self-revelation. Human existence in each epoch is a destiny (*Schicksal*), or in Heidegger's parlance, a "destining" (*Geschick*) "sent," as it were, to Dasein from Being. Technological civilization is one such *Geschick* (*FNT*, 25/24). It is both the "supreme danger" with which Dasein is faced (*FNT*, 27/26) but can also be its "saving power" (*FNT*, 29/28).

39 *SZ*, 175,176/220.
40 *FNT*, 21/20: "En-framing means the gathering together (*Versammelnde*) of that setting upon which sets upon man, i.e., challenges him forth to reveal the real, in the mode of ordering, as standing-reserve. En-framing means that way of revealing which holds sway in the essence of modern technology. . . ."

The "supreme danger" seems obvious enough. It lies in the frenzy to order, regulate and secure nature as raw material. In doing so, technology not only obliterates its own essence as a *Ge-stell* of Being; it obliterates all differences in kind within nature and blinds us to our own essential *humanitas*. The essence of human being lies not in the free exercise of individual volition, nor in this or that project of Dasein (whether scientific, political, moral) but in the fact that in a certain sense Being needs Dasein in order to reveal or conceal itself.

But technology as the ultimate danger can also save man. How? It does so by forcing us to "look into" the ambiguous "essence" of technology. That is, the apparently unstoppable force of technological world-mastery impresses upon our consciousness that here is something which cannot be countered by merely human activity because it was not the product of human agency in the first place. It is the frame within which agency is exercised. And this realization can cause the process to reverse itself. Man is given "entry into that which, of himself, he can neither invent nor in any way make" (*FNT*, 32/31). One might call this Heidegger's version of Nietzsche's diagnosis that the only possible course for humanity is forward into nihilism, in order to emerge, trans-formed, on the far shore.[41]

Or rather, it could just as well be called Heidegger's aesthetic appropriation of Platonic *anamnêsis*. Technology forces man to "recollect" (*FNT*, 33/32) that his essence is granted by Being; by means of this he comes to realize his "innermost indestructible belongingness" to Being; he is recalled, as it were, to his true des-tiny, or highest dignity, as the safe-keeper of truth's revelation (ibid), the "shepherd" of Being. "Saving" is *einholen ins Wesen*, "retrieving something into its essence" (*FNT*, 29/28).[42]

Here, as elsewhere in Heidegger, we come to the role of art.

---

41 Nietzsche, *Wille Zur Macht*, paragraphs, 3, 7, 22–23, 39, 40, 55, 112. And cf., *AWP*, 153 (Appendix 11).

42 William Lovitt's translation of *einholen* as "fetching something home" is also on the mark in emphasizing the element of return, of coming home to an origin from which one had set out.

The path out of the last decadence of the humanistic-metaphysical world picture is negotiated through artistic *poiêsis*, which is "kindred" (*verwandt*) to technology (FNT, 36/35) in its character as a "producing" or bringing-forth. Unlike technology, however, it does not set upon the truth but rather allows it to manifest itself in a "splendor" (*FNT*, 36/34) utterly beyond mere instrumentality. Art is a *technê* that points beyond technology. It is neither entertainment, nor *l'art pour l'art*, nor a subordinate department of the ministry of culture. Art too, is a form of *alêtheuein*, a "bringing-forth of the true into the beautiful" (*FNT*, 35/34). In recalling man to the "highest dignity of his essence" art reveals its "highest possibility" (*FNT*, 36/35), its "saving power."

Just as in the *Phaedrus*, then, where beauty is the only hyper-uranian Form still visible to souls in their fallen and embodied state (there is, Socrates says, no "shine in the images here on earth of justice and moderation and the other things honorable for souls" (*Phdr.*, 250b1–5)) – in Heidegger, too, the beautiful is a gateway, in this case a gateway from this or that epochal "frame" back to the true relation to Being.[43]

To call this "Heideggerian *anamnêsis*" can be misleading without the details. More specifically, I am not concerned with either attacking or substantiating an epistemological position according to which the ability to know anything about particulars of genesis in this life depends upon knowledge of the Ideas of such particulars acquired in a previous one. As Rosen points out (114), following Leibniz, that would be the philosophical equivalent of kicking the problem upstairs without solving it since we still require an account of how Ideas were grasped in the previous incarnation. Rather, recollection is a retrospective realization that stable intelligibility underlies our ability to identify particulars (ibid). By reflection on what it means to think something determinate, we realize, or recollect the necessary likeness or openness of

---

43 See Heidegger's own interpretation of the *Phaedrus* in N, I, 228/196: ". . . it is the beautiful that snatches from the oblivion of Being and grants the view upon Being."

the mind to the objects of knowledge. This is, moreover, precisely the sense which Heidegger gives to Platonic *anamnêsis*: thinking any determinate being occurs within an already existing understanding of *Sein*, to which we return by reflecting on how we think *Seienden*.[44]

For our purposes, what is important is how the relationship of beauty to other Ideas is presented in Plato. In the *Phaedrus*, recollection is through beauty to the *ousia ontôs ousa*, the being which truly is. From there however, the soul is led onward to justice itself (*autên dikaiosunên*), moderation and knowledge and the other *ontôs onta*.[45] In the *Meno*, too, it is the soul's recollection that "all nature is akin," and that it is linked to this totality which is the condition for the ability to "recollect about virtue."[46] Beauty can serve as a point of access for the soul into an interlinked totality of forms because *it* itself is akin to them.

The same is true in Diotima's erotic ladder. Each step of the young initiate's ascent, instigated by physical beauty, leads to a broadening of his conception of the beautiful. One is led from love of a particular beautiful body to love of universal beauty in all bodies, from love of beautiful bodies to psychic beauty, which far outlasts bodily bloom. From there the initiate proceeds to the superior lovability of the "pursuits and laws" which are responsible, across many lifetimes, for the formation of beautiful souls, and from there to the sciences, whose objects are the most universal and not subject to time. At the end, one turns to the single philosophical science of the beautiful *kath'auto*. The manifestation of beauty at each stage is thus "higher" than the preceding one by being more encompassing

---

44 *MAL*, 185–185/147–148. Something along the same lines underlies Hegel's high estimation of the *anamnêsis* myths as portraying the "true nature of consciousness." See *Vorlesungen über die Geschichte der Philosophie*, II, 43–44.

45 *Phdr.* 247c5–e3.

46 *Men.*, 81c9–d2: "Seeing as all nature is akin, and the soul has learned all things, there is nothing that prevents someone who recollects (which people call learning) one thing only from discovering all things."

and also by greater temporal endurance. In other words, beauty is linked to ("reminds" us of) universality, comprehensiveness and eternity.[47]

And lest we chalk this up to the histrionic atmosphere of the so-called erotic dialogues, substantially the same point is made in the relentlessly "sober" *Philebus* where recollection is not a theme. The good in the *Philebus* "dwells," not somewhere beyond being, but within the "beautifully mixed" life.[48] The beautiful mixture, however, is constituted by *telos,* measure, order and harmony, and these cannot be understood without a study of the ontological structure of pure form and the eidetic "henads" (i.e., the One and the Many, or Limit and the Unlimited).[49] This underlies Socrates' claim that the study of formal intelligibility, or the very fact that all things which are, are out of the One and the Many, is a "beautiful road" sent to man by the gods.[50] Through limit, measure and harmony, beauty is linked to the ordered structure of *eidos* and hence to the intellect. But as we know from the *Republic*, *idea* and *nous* are both further "yoked" to the Good.[51]

Can the aesthetic play the same role in Heidegger? Clearly, he wishes to retain the recollective impact of non-utilitarian beauty. The difficulty Heidegger notes is that the *kosmos noêtos* recollected in Platonic *anamnêsis* is understood according to a certain governing time-concept (namely, enduring presence). According to Heidegger, Plato even had an inkling that this was the case. Describing the relation of *psuchê* to Being as re-collection (i.e., of something in the *past*, or in a *previous* existence) implies the link between Being and Time, but only mythically.[52] Plato did not see that if Being is related to Dasein, then determinations that some beings are "in time" (natural

---

47   Even Alcibiades sees this link between beauty, truth and comprehensiveness. He admits that Socrates' speeches cover the *whole* area which must be known if one is to be beautiful and good. *Symp.* 222a5.

48   *Phlb.* 61b7–8.

49   Cf. *Phlb.* 20d1–5 with 64d1–e8.

50   Ibid., 16b6.

51   *R.* 507d11–508a2.

52   *MAL,* 187/148.

or historical beings) and some beings are "out of" time, or "above" time (say Ideas), are all modes derivative of Dasein's temporality, which has been left completely unexamined.[53]

Unlike Platonic *psuchê*, then, Heideggerean Dasein does not recall an eternal horizon of intelligibility. Rather, man is reminded of the overwhelming power of the archaic Greek encounter with Being. At the dawn of the West, Being was experienced as *phusis*, a kinetic process or event in which beings emerge from and return to concealment, rendered in Heidegger's German as *das Walten*: "the emerging-abiding sway." *Phusis* is "the event of standing forth, arising from the concealed and thus enabling the concealed to take its stand . . ." (*IM*, 17/16). Being in this sense is prior to its later disjunction from becoming, appearance, and thinking. It is also prior to the later Platonic-Aristotelian conception of "scientific" *logos* which stands over Being and judges it or predicates about it. Primordially, *logos* is not rational or scientific speech, but the articulation of the kinetic unity of *phusis* itself (*EM*, 139/138).[54] This kinetic unity, as we have already remarked, can only come to presence in a being such as Dasein.[55] Since, like Being, Dasein is temporally constituted, the object of its *anamnêsis* must also be temporal – the origin of the *Seinsgeschichte*.

As Heidegger argues at length in his *Introduction to Metaphysics*, however, the delicate balance of this origin *could not* be maintained. Dasein had to "fall away" from it. History is also the forgetting of Being,[56] which continues, it would seem, until the restorative catastrophe of nihilism opens the possibility of a return. The "truth" then, which art brings forth is what Heidegger calls "the dialogue of divine and human *Geschicken*" (*FNT*,

---

53 *MAL*, 184/146.
54 *See EM*, 141/141: Being "is not a heap or pile"; it is characterized by "rank and dominance."
55 *EM*, 171–72/174. And cf. *EM* 155/156ff for Heidegger's interpretation of the choral ode in *Antigone*.
56 *EM*, 187/190 and 194/198: "Transformation of being from *phusis* to *idea* itself brings about one of the essential forms of movement within the history of the West, not only of its art."

35/34). In other words, even within the uttermost planetary nihilism, art provides a vision of the *totality* of our historical fate which rejuvenates by recalling the greatness of the historical origin, in which Dasein was the receptive witness to Being.

Stated in the most general terms, then, Heidegger looks to the origin for the same reason that Socrates turns to the Ideas: he wants to know how, or with what, one can live intelligently, knowing where one stands.[57] The Ideas do not provide for any simple reconciliation of theory, practice and *poiêsis*. But for those rare individuals dominated by theoretical eros, the "recollection" of the Ideas allows them to understand, retrospectively, what they were doing their whole lives. The eternal horizon recollects temporal life into a coherent picture, for at least some people, some of the time.[58]

The Heideggerian *Denker*, too, wants to understand what he is doing. He wants to understand nihilism for example and thus overcome it, after a fashion. In trying to think his way back to the origin of Western philosophy, he tries to transcend this or that *Geschick*, in order to understand the fate of Being as a whole. Even the technological *Ge-stell* is never simply "blind destiny" or "completely ordained fate." The "truth of Being" illuminates it if we know where to look.[59]

The understanding of fate as whole is not merely comprehensive however; it also implies a kind of superiority. Art, in recalling Dasein to its true role, reveals "the highest dignity of his [man's] essence,"[60] which implies a link between aesthetic beauty, comprehensiveness of understanding, and the rank-order of kinds of possible life. But what exactly is the status of such a rank-ordering? And how is it grounded in the origin of *Seinsgeschichte*?

---

57 See *WdW*, 209/150–151 on Dasein's need for *Bodenständigkeit*, a "ground-stance." And cf. *HB*, 357/274: "The truth of being offers a hold for all comportment (*Den Halt für alles Verhalten*)."

58 Cf. *R.* 505d11–e1and *Symp.* 210e5–6.

59 *K*, 122/47.

60 *FNT*, 33/32 and cf. *K*,118/42.

Here things become obscure. That origin is "great" or "inceptive" by virtue of the whole history to which it gives birth – the necessary history of Being's self-concealing manifestations and Dasein's fall.[61] To return to the origin of history, then, means to begin that same history again, with the fall away from the origin and everything that must follow from it. The origin cannot be an absolute moment outside of or "higher" than the history of which it is the origin. But where then does the rank order of "better" or "higher" modes of Dasein's comportment come from? On what ground is it greater, or more beautiful, or more in keeping with Dasein's "way of being," to live in full knowledge of fate, rather than in total ignorance? The origin itself cannot teach us this, nor can reflection on history, since Being's manifestations and occlusions are both equiprimordial, constituent elements *of* that history.

And there is another question. In coming to realize the true relationship of technology to Being, Dasein does not step up out of history. It simply readies itself to face the next, temporally finite and contingent epoch of Being, the "arrival" of which is a destiny (*Schicksal*) which it awaits, but does not control.[62] The understanding that this is the case, however, is supposed to be available no matter the epoch, as is the link between beauty and Dasein's "ownmost" way of being as the shepherd of *Sein*.

Which, then, really *is* the fundamental horizon? Is the understanding of the being of such things as the beautiful or the good bounded by the historical "gifts," the pulsations of Being in this or that *Geschick* or epoch? Perhaps. But then in what sense can artistic *poiêsis* serve as a gateway *between* epochs of history? And how are we to understand the implicit (or not so implicit) appeal to a trans-epochal interrelation between beauty, goodness and comprehensive understanding (or the goodness and nobility of

---

61 *EM*, 199/ 204: "The ground of the collapse lies first in the greatness of the inception and in the essence of the inception itself. . . . The inception must, as incipient, in a certain way leave itself behind."
62 *FNT,* 25–26/24–25 and *K,* 115–116/37–38.

comprehensive understanding) which "recalls" Dasein to its essence? It seems to be the case – despite Heidegger's frequent assertions to the contrary – that historical epochs are distinguished, characterized and *ranked*, in other words, that time in its existential significance, is understood in the light of *something else* – an interrelation of intelligible forms or natures, and that *these* would be the horizon within which Dasein's temporality obtains its distinctive character.

In other words, in seeking to understand man's late modern predicament, Heidegger continues to rely on a web of conceptual relations drawn from the metaphysics of presence, or Platonism. By themselves, such Platonic echoes are neither surprising nor even fatal for Heidegger's project. After all, by a "*Destruktion*" of metaphysics Heidegger never meant to plow it under and pour salt over the ground. Rather, he aimed to re-expose its roots or foundations as part of a search for what they conceal.[63] The goal is obviously to translate such "metaphysical" concepts into a temporal-historical horizon, but it is not clear that the translation can be carried through without remainder.

Though I can only note it in passing, this situation seems to me to transcend the much-discussed *Kehre,* or turn, from Heidegger's early to his later thought. Whether we approach Being through the existential analytic of Dasein or by passive meditation on *Seinsgeschichte,* the problem is the same – how to articulate the *Ursprünglichkeit,* the "primordiality" of temporality.

In *Being and Time* the tension appears as the question of whether authentic existence and resoluteness (*Entschlossenheit*) are acts of Dasein, something it can (or must) do, or an "event" which happens to it. Authenticity, of course, can only be grasped in relation to death (*SZ, 234/277*). What is unclear is how exactly, and why, the encounter with the fact of death moves Dasein from inauthenticity to authenticity.

---

63 *EM,* 125/124 on the primordial overcoming (*ursprünglich überwinden*) of the division between Being and Thinking, which allows a refounding of its truth (presumably upon new ground).

Sometimes, the move is described as an act or choice, a possibility which Dasein takes upon itself.[64] In other places, it seems to be a transformation in comportment necessitated through, or constituted by, a sudden *Augenblick*, a "moment of vision" which "shatters" (*SZ*, 129/167) everyday inauthentic existence and forces Dasein willy-nilly to see inauthenticity for what it is – thrown, "factic" existence (*SZ* 307–308/355).

The *Augenblick* retains unmistakable echoes of the Platonic *periagogê*, the "turning round of the soul," or of the *exaiphnês*, the sudden moment of illumination which constitutes the non-discursive step to the Ideas. In this case, however, Dasein sees or becomes "transparent" to itself. In Plato, it is the turn from Becoming to Being which begins the philosopher's journey from dreams to wakefulness.[65] In Heidegger the *Augenblick*, the turn from inauthenticity to authenticity, accounts for the unity and connectedness of the self.[66]

But again, in the *Augenblick* Dasein does not leave, or even remake, this world. The only thing that "occurs" is Dasein's vision of a difference between constancy and distraction (*Zerstreuung*) or between clarity of vision and "lostness" (*Verlorenheit*) (*SZ*, 390/442). Where does this difference come from? It cannot be from the fact of death. Death is the "measureless possibility of the impossibility of existence." It gives Dasein "nothing to actualize," nothing which "Dasein, as actual could itself be" (*SZ*, 262/307). Being mute, death gives no instructions. Indeed, it could not point to the superiority of a life of full self-knowledge as opposed to illusion, or to the superiority of constancy (*Ständigkeit*) as opposed to dissolution. This would imply that one comportment was higher in dignity or importance, more worthy of being actualized, than another. But this is impossible, since it would undermine the predominance of possibility and *Geworfenheit* in the analysis of

---

64 Cf., *SZ* 42/68, 263–264/308, 268/313.
65 *R.* 534c–d.
66 *SZ*, 390–391/442–443, and cf. *SZ*, 299/346: ". . . resoluteness is what first gives authentic transparency to Dasein."

Dasein.[67] And yet the distinction between authenticity and its opposite, however understood, requires Dasein to see the difference between them *as a distinction of rank* between certain ways of life, or between *kalos* and *aischros,* and make the connection between "beautiful" and "true," in this case its "true" selfhood as unified, constant, loyal, self-standing, resolute.[68] But the content of the distinction cannot emerge either from authentic "Being-toward-Death" or authentic comportment to the future. It is presupposed by the difference between these and inauthenticity.

The question of Being, says Heidegger, can only be addressed to Dasein.[69] Dasein however, is not a "what" or a fixed essence. It is a "who," a "way" of being (*SZ,* 114–117/150–153). To be a "who," however, means nothing less than to exist either authentically or inauthentically.[70] If we cannot explain how Dasein moves from one to the other, then its "who-ness" loses all coherence. But if this is so then the path to any fundamental understanding of temporality is blocked since Heidegger insists that "primordial" temporality is seen *only* in Dasein's authentic comportment to the future (i.e., its authentic Being-toward-death): *"Temporality is experienced in a phenomenally primordial way in Dasein's authentic Being-a-whole, in . . . anticipatory resoluteness."*[71]

A great deal more needs to be said about all this which must be left unsaid here. For now, the outline of the whole difficulty

---

67 *SZ,* 143–144/183: "Possibility as an *existentiale* is the most primordial and ultimate, positive ontological determination of Dasein." Of course, Heidegger does not mean here possibility as indeterminacy or *libertas indifferentiae.* He means possibility as *Geworfenheit* – always being thrown into some definite possibility. But "thrown possibility" is one thing, *energeia* is something else altogether. Cf. *SZ,* 233/276.

68 *WdW,* 198/143: "Only someone who is *inwardly* gathered and connected" is capable of *kalôs legein.* On resoluteness and loyalty (*Treue*) see *SZ,* 391/443.

69 *SZ,* 7/27 and 12/32.

70 *SZ,* 325/372.

71 *SZ,* 304/351. And cf. SZ, 13/34: "Therefore, *fundamental ontology,* from which alone all other ontologies arise, must be sought in the *existential analytic of Dasein*" [emphases are Heidegger's]. The same is true of History, or the "historicality" (*Geschichtlichkeit*) of Dasein (SZ, 386/438).

will have to suffice: If there are distinctions between modes of comportment or between epochs of history, and if those distinctions *move* Dasein, are in some sense determinative or normative for it or for the Heideggerian *Denker*, then time or history constantly point to standards of evaluation and judgment which elucidate the temporal horizon, which give it its character as the temporality *of* Dasein (rather than mere chronological succession or "clock time"), but are not explicable within it. We try to interpret ourselves temporally, but there is always a nagging suspicion that we are using tools smuggled in from somewhere else.

Once again, the *chorismos* between time and eternity, the basic problem of Platonic thought, proves to be no mere relic of the ancient ontological concern with ultimate first principles, origins, or "what is always." Even if we resolutely turn away from such ontology, the problem, in some form or another, is still staring at our backs. I offer this to the reader as a vivid example of Stanley Rosen's remark that Platonic thought is a firebird, constantly being reborn from the ashes of refutation.[72]

---

72 Rosen, *Question of Being*, ix.

Lecture One:
Aristotelianizing Plato

It is a great honor to be invited to deliver a series of lectures dedicated to the memory of Etienne Gilson. At the same time, one feels intimidated by the shadow of Gilson's erudition and extraordinary accomplishments. For this reason, I prefer to think that the honor accrues to Gilson himself, whom we acknowledge by our presence together under the friendly auspices of the Institut Catholique. In a more fundamental sense, perhaps we can say that Gilson and we are united in our desire to honor metaphysics. Despite the uncertain meaning of the term, and the consequent variety in the conceptions and motives that lead us to honor her, our very unity, and indeed, the continuous presence of something called metaphysics for more than two millennia, demonstrates that our enterprise is not entirely quixotic.

For my part, I am not surprised or discouraged by the peculiar history of metaphysics or the etymological ambiguity of the name itself. Why should a way of thinking and speaking that presumes to treat the most fundamental and so comprehensive problems of human experience have enjoyed a unified, or shall we say a clear and distinct, historical development? The multiple personality of metaphysics stems directly from the fact that it is explicitly and unashamedly concerned with questions that are not susceptible of determinate answers, but which press in upon us by our very natural dissatisfaction with determinate answers as such. We do not need to define metaphysics at the outset of our inquiries because it is metaphysics that defines us.

In that sense, I agree with Heidegger that metaphysics is the destiny of our western civilization. In saying this, of course, I do not accept his narrow and over-simplified definition of the term. On the contrary, the multiplicity of metaphysical doctrines shows the wisdom of Nietzsche's observation that man is the not yet completed or fully finished being. Stated very generally, metaphysics is the incomplete, anticipatory reflection upon what it would be to be complete. This is a reflection that invokes not ourselves alone but what philosophers from Plato to Heidegger have called "the whole." As my teacher Leo Strauss used to say, human being is that part of the whole that is open to the whole.[1] Unfortunately, whereas we are open to the whole, in another sense we are closed to it. The part that is open to the whole remains a part.

Metaphysics has been subjected to sharp criticism from many quarters. Its ambiguity is well demonstrated by the fact that the two predominant criticisms in the late modern epoch are mutually contradictory. The first protests that metaphysics lacks clarity and distinctness; the second holds on the contrary that metaphysics, as introduced by Plato, has concealed genuine thinking by the desire for clarity and distinctness. To exaggerate somewhat for introductory purposes, metaphysics is accused on the one hand of the depreciation of mathematics and on the other of a surrender to it. The accusers thus agree that the locus of the deficiencies of metaphysics is that of exactness. And this seems to transform the problem into one of method. But the two types of criticism

---

1   [Editor's Note: Since the full quote from Strauss bears directly on Rosen's concerns and on Heidegger's, I reproduce it in full: "The unity of man consists in the fact that he is that part of the whole which is open to the whole, or, in Platonic language, that part of the whole which has seen the ideas of all things. Man's concern with his openness to the whole is the life of the mind. The dualism of being a part while being open to the whole, and therefore in a sense being the whole itself, is man." Leo Strauss, "The Problem of Socrates," in *The Rebirth of Classical Political Rationalism* (Chicago: University of Chicago Press, 1989), 164.]

disagree on the interpretation of the preferred meaning of "method." For the first type, method is the articulation of exactness, closely allied with if not the same as mathematics. Method is thus technical in two senses. It is a rule-governed activity that is grounded in an antecedent conception of the structure of experience. As such, it produces artifacts of intelligibility, such as equations and models, which provide us with a symbolic representation of the order of the world. In the ideal case, a sound method furnishes us with a decision procedure for verifying or invalidating the propositions in the representation.

To call this representation "ultimate reality" is to reduce human experience to an illusion. But mathematical construction is also a human "project," as we say today. Despite its extraordinary power, mathematics is not strong enough to withstand the charge that it too is subordinate to the human will. Contemporary talk about non-standard arithmetic and deviant logic, to say nothing of non-Euclidean geometry, n-dimensional space, and the paradoxes of quantum mechanics, could lead one to believe that the mathematician's paradise is not entirely Platonist but dangerously Nietzschean. Exactness is apparently compatible with perspectivism. This is already suggested by the mathematician Kronecker's remark that God created the natural numbers, whereas man has created all the rest of mathematics. As is perhaps especially evident from the contemporary discussions of cosmologists, the road of exactness leads back into the heart of metaphysics, and if I may say so, to a post-modern metaphysics.

For the second type of anti-metaphysical argument, as exemplified by Heidegger, the preferred sense of method is the more literal one of being "on the way" (*unterwegs*). If we cannot quite define the direction in which we are moving, this is because the road or path leads us away from, that is, behind, beneath, and above, exactness. We can however say that this critique of metaphysics rebukes her for replacing the original conception of truth as unconcealedness with the paradigm of correctness. Otherwise stated, the charge here is that truth ceases to be regarded as a property of beings and becomes instead a property of conceptual discourse, as is obvious from emphasis upon the doctrine of predication, which in turn leads to the concept of the truth predicate. What began as *mathesis universalis* has been transformed into the metaphysics of production, thanks to the development in our conception of mathematics as a creative enterprise.[2]

I express this Heideggerian thesis, which, if it is not formulated by him in so many words, certainly follows from his version of the history of philosophy, as that of the decay of metaphysics from substance to syntax. The expression can be justified by noticing that metaphysics has survived its deconstruction by phenomenology and hermeneutics primarily among contemporary analytical philosophers. It is now legitimate and even fashionable to speak of analytical metaphysics. Its practitioners belong for the most part to the formalist wing of the analytical movement and have returned to metaphysics as a result of technical issues in logic and more broadly, the philosophy of science. If we look through the many contributions to analytical metaphysics of the past quarter-century, we could well imagine ourselves to be in the midst of a revival of scholasticism. The old problems – being, nothing, existence, predication, universals – are once more in full bloom, although bedizened with the cosmetics of mathematical logic, set theory, and more recently, neurophysiology. This shows us that the very methods that failed to extirpate traditional metaphysics are now being used to sustain her revivification. Analytical metaphysics is re-enacting the Kantian dialectic between a repudiation of metaphysics and a recognition of its enduring existence, albeit in different forms. But its emphasis upon the creativity of formalist thinking is a post-Kantian innovation.

I suppose that Heidegger would assimilate my account of analytical metaphysics into his interpretation of modern technology. There is an intimate connection within the heart of analytical metaphysics between the construction of formal models of

---

2   For an exemplary statement of the evolution of doctrines of truth into the philosophy of language, see Heidegger's 1942/43 seminar *Parmenides* (*GA,* 54, especially 49/33–34, 72/49ff and 102/69.

metaphysical discourse and the thesis of metaphysical productionism that Heidegger finds at the heart of Platonism. I cite as an important example the Quinean doctrine of the indeterminacy of translation, as well as his famous assertion that to be is to be the value of a variable in an interpretation of a quantified proposition in the first-order predicate calculus. The first thesis leads directly to the conception of the production of rational order by linguistic decisions; in the second thesis, the key term is "interpretation," which is supplied by the empirical and mathematical sciences.

Quine would not speak of metaphysics but rather of the philosophy of language or logic. More precisely, he would refer to the logical clarification of existence statements that are verified by the empirical sciences. This does not contradict my point, since it is the precise purpose of philosophical logic to replace metaphysics. In other words, Being is replaced by existence, and what exists is a consequence of human decisions concerning how to speak in the most exact way possible. One might characterize Quine's innovation in non-Quinean terms by calling it a shift from ontology to existentialism, or even to decisionism. Since the decision is itself formulated by a faith in logical analysis, Quine's position is circular, but that does not alter its metaphysical implications. The world is a linguistic product of the scientific attempt to master nature and revise her in the image of our desires. But these desires are themselves conditioned by our linguistic habits. This is what I mean by the shift from substance to syntax.

If this is right, then we can say that one of the two major contemporary critiques of metaphysics has been transformed by its own technical exertions into a new version of metaphysics. The new metaphysics is in part a continuation of traditional Platonism, to the extent that it pursues mathematical or formal structure. But to the extent that these structures are produced on the authority of modern science, the new metaphysics is Platonism *à la* Heidegger. As it turns out, by studying Heidegger's critique of metaphysics or Platonism, we are also studying the foundations of contemporary analytical metaphysics.

In sum: from a Heideggerian standpoint, the contemporary version of what I shall call the quarrel between discovery and production is an exhibition of a fissure within Platonism that was not consciously understood by Plato and which gave rise to the history of metaphysics. Mathematics turns into poetry. In more brutal language, poetry itself deteriorates into the ideology of *technê*. There can be no doubt that the general tendency of Heidegger's account of this transformation is defensible, however we may disagree with the details. Nevertheless, I continue to believe that the initial step in Heidegger's history of metaphysics is misleading, and at key points mistaken. The major error is not to discern a dimension of productionism in Plato, but to mislocate its position within the Platonic teaching. I also see considerable difficulty in Heidegger's treatment of the relation between Plato and Aristotle, which I shall discuss shortly. This has serious consequences for Heidegger's monolithic account of Platonism as extending throughout the entire history of western philosophy.

All questions of error to one side, I shall take my bearings by certain aspects of Heidegger's account of Platonism because of its great influence, and more importantly, because the attempt to come to grips with Heidegger has helped me to understand Plato. In addition to the relation between Plato and Aristotle, I shall be discussing in these lectures two other topics: (1) the attribution to Plato of a conception of truth and Being as full presence of that which is fully and always, and (2) the claim that Plato arrives at a doctrine of Being as "producedness" under the influence of the model of the artisan or craftsman. The connection between the two topics should be obvious. If Socrates defines Being as that which is fully present to the eye of the soul as that which is always, then production is excluded from ontology. The central question is then whether Platonism is accurately understood as advocating unqualifiedly the thesis of *parousia*, and, of course, if it does not, whether this is enough to commit Plato to a metaphysics of production.

Before I turn to the Aristotelianizing of Plato, it will be helpful to remind you as simply as possible how Heidegger formulates the issue of production. Speaking with reference to the discussion of the Idea of the bed in Book Ten of the *Republic*, Heidegger cites Socrates' assertion that god wanted to be the genuine maker of the genuine bed, which, once having been produced, will serve as the paradigm for all beds subsequently manufactured by human craftsmen. Heidegger concludes as follows:

> In what is then for Plato the essence of the Idea and therewith of Being finally grounded? In the fastening together of producing [*in der Ansetzung eines Schaffenden*], the essentiality of which appears to be produced only then, when its production is unique, a one, by which one can account for that superelevation from the representation of a multiplicity to the representation of its unity.[3]

Heidegger is of course well aware of the fact that Plato normally describes the Ideas as *aei on*, "always present." But he replies to this that the model of the craftsman is the implicit presupposition for all notions of producedness, and that (to quote from an earlier text) "What is not in need of being produced can really be understood and discovered only within the understanding of Being that goes with production." And again: "In production therefore we encounter directly that which does not require to be produced."[4] There is a central lacuna in this thesis. No reason is given as to why being (or Being) must itself be produced, merely because it is our experience of production that prepares us to think the unproduced. Another very general example of the same unjustified form of reasoning is to be found in Heidegger's reliance upon etymologies. Simply because *ousia* originally means "wealth" or material substance, it hardly follows that Aristotle confused being with money. Nor does the ocular root of *eidos* or *idea* require us to look for Plato's controlling insight in the *technê* of optics.

---

3   *N,* I, 213/183–184.
4   *GPP,* 163/116.

One last example: it does not follow from the temporal senses of *on* and *einai* that doctrines of everlasting being are compromised or contradicted by their own testimony. To say that they are is like arguing that the original meaning of "ground" in German is enough to show that Hegel was a materialist. This characteristic of Heidegger's teaching reminds one of the late Wittgenstein, or even better, John Austin's endless etymologizing in an effort to cast ridicule upon metaphysics in favor of so-called ordinary language.

To come back to production, we can offer a partial but suggestive defense of Heidegger by noting that Socrates himself refers occasionally to the Ideas as produced, in particular when he is using poetic or rhetorical language. In order to retain what I will call the standard Platonist position, and certainly if one hopes to develop a deeper or non-standard interpretation of Plato, one must address the appearance of a productionist doctrine of Being. As mentioned previously, I begin with the assistance of Aristotle. The general point is perhaps this: Even though Aristotle is viewed by Heidegger as making a technical advance over Plato, the fundamental concepts of the two thinkers are held to be expressions of the same metaphysics. The net result is that Heidegger is led into two mutually inconsistent approaches to Plato. He is sensitive to the importance of Plato's myths and to the poetical presentations of metaphysical doctrines, but he also contends that we must approach Plato by way of Aristotle, who explicitly criticizes the use of myths in philosophy.

I will expand this point in a moment, but first, an informal remark. It is rather evident that Heidegger is not at ease with the Platonic dialogues, as he certainly is, for example, with Aristotle and Kant. If I may refer to oral tradition, H. G. Gadamer once told me of Heidegger's admission that he had never understood Plato. The same remark could correctly be made by many others, but in the case of the importance that Heidegger places upon his version of Platonism, the remark becomes especially interesting. I suggest that the reason for Heidegger's discomfort is a lack of playfulness. There are frequent bitter remarks but few if any jokes in the Heideggerian corpus, whereas seriousness and solemnity are all too frequently exaggerated to the point of the ponderous and the melodramatic.

I was once criticized by a Heideggerian for alluding in a public lecture to her master's humorlessness as a writer, on the grounds that the charge, even if true, was personal and had nothing to do with his qualities as a thinker. I am afraid that I cannot agree. We Platonists subscribe to the sentiments of the Athenian Stranger who, in Book Seven of the *Laws*, tells us that god alone is a serious matter whereas human things are not. The latter should be treated with a noble playfulness, not, as one can say, with ontological grimness or *Angst vor dem Tode*. As the Stranger also puts it, we are forced to be serious about the human, but great seriousness is due the god only.[5] I cannot here attempt an extensive exegesis of this passage. Suffice it to say that enforced seriousness is for the sake of noble playfulness, just as war is for the sake of peace.

This point has to be borne in mind at all times when reading the Platonic dialogues. It helps to explain why Plato wrote dialogues, or as we say in English, "plays." But we have to distinguish between two senses of "play." In the games that children (or adults) play, we may or may not pretend to be someone else. In a drama, however, this pretense is obvious and essential. Plato's dialogues are not games like chess or soccer; they are dramas. As such, they obey the Heideggerian conception of truth to the extent that they conceal their meanings, which must be "torn" (*entrissen*) or liberated from the darkness in order to bring them forth into the light.[6] And, just as Heidegger observes of the original view of truth, the darkness continues to play its role in the truth itself. I

---

5 *Lg.,* VII, 803b3–c8).
6 Martin Heidegger, *GBM*, 43/29: "Die Wahrheit wird von den Griechen als ein Raub verstanden, der der Verborgenheit entrissen werden muss in einer Auseinandersetzung, in der gerade die *phusis* danach strebt, sich zu verbergen." [Ed. – "Truth is understood by the Greeks as something stolen, which must be torn from concealment in a confrontation in which precisly *phusis* strives to conceal itself."]

will concentrate upon this point in subsequent lectures. Here I want to say that Aristotle is not the best preparation for understanding this side of Plato's dialogues.

Of equal importance is the fact that the Platonic dialogues are populated by human beings, not by phenomenological descriptions of ontological activity. Without exaggerating the point, it is evident that Aristotle is closer to Heidegger in this respect. In Aristotle's treatise *On the Soul*, no human beings are mentioned and in the *Nicomachean Ethics*, if I am not mistaken, there is just one example of a virtuous person, namely, Pericles. At least in these two works, Aristotle finds it possible to speak about human life without invoking living human beings, whereas Plato does not. Regardless of which approach we may prefer, our first task is to perceive the difference.

If I may borrow a term from Heidegger, that difference is fundamentally ontological, not simply a matter of literary style. Plato and Aristotle have quite different ways of discussing what Heidegger calls the existential analysis of *Dasein*. It is a theoretical error of the highest significance to suppress this difference by conceiving of Plato as a simpler, less technically adroit precursor of Aristotle. But this is in effect what Heidegger does in his major works from the *Sophist* lectures through *Being and Time* to *Introduction to Metaphysics*. Not only, he says, can we assume that Aristotle understood Plato, but it is also the case that the student is a more radical and scientific version of the master. The successors always understand their predecessors better than they understood themselves. In short, there is no access to Plato except through Aristotle.[7] And this is true, not because Aristotle devised a newer and more penetrating doctrine, but because he makes

---

7   *PS*, 11/8, 189/131, 199/138. [Ed.: Page 11 of the *Sophist* lectures contains an especially clear statement of Heidegger's interpretative principle. He even goes so far as to identify the route from Aristotle back to Plato with the route from "the clear into the obscure" (*vom Hellen ins Dunkle gehen soll*). He also frankly confesses that he will make the "presupposition" (*Voraussetzung*) that Aristotle understood Plato, and understood him better than Plato understood himself.]

Platonism more radical and more scientific, or as we can also say, clearer and more distinct.[8] One wonders whether Heidegger would agree that the best way to approach his own work is via Derrida or Gadamer.

This strand of Heidegger's evaluation is especially odd because it seems to go against a deeper appreciation on his part for poetical thinking as contrasted with the technical terminology of the rationalist philosophical tradition. We see this preference, not merely in the interpretations of Hölderlin or Trakl, but especially in the studies devoted to the pre-Socratic "thinkers," a term used to designate their special profundity as contrasted with mere "philosophers" (alias metaphysicians). One receives from Heidegger the distinct (but not unqualified) impression that Plato himself reaches the level of "thinker" in his myths and allegories, a level no doubt flawed by the metaphysics of production or the preference for the light of the Ideas to that of Being, but nevertheless superior to Plato's discursive ratiocination.

It is also important to note that, by seeing Aristotle as a technically superior version of Plato, Heidegger veils from his own view the many ways in which he is himself closer to Plato than to Aristotle. He aligns himself with the partisans of exactness in a way that is both at odds with his critique of metaphysics and contradicted by his choice of allegories or myths as proof-texts for his reading of Plato. There is also a disharmony between a preference for successors and the deep Heideggerian impetus to return to the origins.

I turn now to a consideration of how Heidegger assimilates Plato into the Aristotelian doctrine of being *qua* being.[9] In order

---

8   Alain Boutot reminds us of Heidegger's preference for Aristotle in the period of *Sein und Zeit* in his *Heidegger et Platon: Le Probleme du Nihilisme* (Paris: Presse Universitaires de France, 1987), 52. My point is that Heidegger's tendency to dissolve the difference between the two Greek thinkers runs side by side with this preference for Aristotle.

9   [Ed.: For a fuller treatment of this issue, see Stanley Rosen, *The Question of Being: A Reversal of Heidegger* (South Bend, Indiana: St. Augustine's Press, 2002), 23–35. (hereinafter *QB*)]

to carry out this goal, I call attention to two important elements of the Aristotelian problematic. In the course of history, one element, the doctrine of categories and predication, is either blended together with or entirely replaces the other, the doctrine of noetic intuition of pure form. The unifying thread of these two main points can be stated as follows. Heidegger interprets Aristotle's doctrine of predication as a kind of scientifically more precise version of Platonist productionism, in which the true nature of Being as the emergence process of beings is concealed by linguistic artifacts or discursive products of how beings look to human cognition. Instead of bespeaking Being, Aristotle and his successors speak of this or that property of beings. As Heidegger puts it, the doctrine of predication, or saying "something about something" (*ti kata tinos*), refers to two "somethings" (*etwas als etwas*) or reifications of Being.[10] This carries with it the corollary that Being is covered over by the view of how it "looks" to us as a this-something.

Perhaps even more important, the doctrine of intellectual intuition (*noêsis*) is itself covered over by discursive analysis. So far as I am aware, Heidegger does not discuss this particular concealment extensively, but the relative obscurity of the doctrine of *noêsis* certainly leads to an exaggeration in the status of discursive thinking (*dianoia*) and gives dominance to the analysis of the structure of intelligibility without due attention to the visibility of what is being analyzed. The same historical evolution can arise from more explicitly Platonist sources, but it is more difficult to subordinate intuition to predication in Plato because of his great emphasis upon the vision of Ideas and his relatively undeveloped doctrine of predication.

Absent the attention to visibility, language tends to become productive or anthropocentric, in keeping with Heidegger's account of the tradition. This tradition could more appropriately be called Aristotelianism than Platonism. Since languages are human artifacts (even the so-called "natural" languages),

10 See esp. *SZ*, 158–59/200–201.

discourse is closer to production than is vision. On this point, it seems to me, Heidegger is at bottom closer to Plato than to Aristotle. His account of the lighting-process of Being, which is later than his studies on *parousia* and production in the *Republic*, reminds us of the Socratic metaphor of the sun and the Idea of the Good in the central books of the *Republic*. Even if it could be shown that Aristotle's technical terms arise from the same underlying metaphysics as Plato's, this would not alter the fact that Heidegger's doctrine employs Platonist rather than Aristotelian language. Another sign of this is the rather Fichtean flavor of a Being that conceals itself through the "mittence" or production of beings.

Of one thing there can be very little doubt. Aristotle is altogether more important than Plato as a source for the development of the philosophy of language in western metaphysics. And this means that the metaphysics of production owes more to Aristotle than to Plato. When the intuition of pure forms is slighted or ignored entirely, language comes to play an unrestricted role in what we call today the construction of reality. The structure of intelligibility is now a mode of discourse. What we say and how we speak thus come to determine the sense of what we see. The step from Proust to Nelson Goodman is much shorter than we might imagine, as the title of Goodman's last book, *Ways of World-Making*, testifies.

Let us now look more closely at the discursive dimension of the science of being qua being. This science does not address itself to the Heideggerian Being that is the origination of all things. Instead, it provides an analytical account of what it is to be a composite natural substance (*sunolon*), of a sort that is grasped by sense-perception as an independent unity. In grammatical terms, the unity is that of a subject and its predicates. Predicates refer to essential and accidental properties. Thus Socrates is a subject that cannot be predicated of something else, but which shows itself as the owner of its properties. The owner is the *sunolon*, not the *eidos*, which latter exhibits the essential properties of the substance, for example, in the case of Socrates, "rational animal."

Aristotle refers to both the *sunolon* and the *eidos* as *ousia*, his word for being in the primary sense.[11] In my opinion there is no evidence for choosing one of these senses as superior to the other; instead, Aristotle indicates a fundamental dualism in the analysis of being. The *eidos* is primary as that which contains the essence of the individual, but essences are not independent entities; they belong to the *sunolon* or compound substance, which as owner of properties, is also primary. It is not possible to reduce one of these senses to the other. And this leads to a conception of being that is fundamentally different from that of the Platonic Idea, assuming with Heidegger that the Idea expresses the fundamental element in Platonic ontology.

The *eidos* is obviously closer in nature to the Platonic Idea than is the *sunolon*, as is evident from the fact that the first two are perceived by *noêsis*. But the science of being qua being is not the science of the Ideas, nor is it the science of *ousia* in the sense of the *eidos*. It is rather the science of a discursive schema, a recipe for what is required of something in order to qualify as a being: namely, to possess an essence (species-form) along with properties that are instances of one or another of the remaining categories. This is the formal structure that must be exhibited by any determinate being whatsoever.[12] The science of being qua being thus presents us with the analysis of how to talk correctly about these determinate beings. Again we see that both types of *ousia*, the concrete individual and the essence, are jointly the basis of the science of being qua being. In the grammatical component of that science, the subject is the equivalent of the concrete *ousia* or substance and the predicates include the *eidos* as well as representatives of the

11 The *sunolon* is featured in the *Categories* and the *eidos* is the preferred sense of *ousia* in *Metaphysics Z*. But this notoriously difficult text also treats the *sunolon* as if it, too, were a legitimate candidate for the principal sense of *ousia*. Attempts to resolve this ambiguity are based upon forced readings of the text, readings which themselves assume a variety of hypotheses, such as that of Aristotle's development and which passages in Z express Aristotle's own current views and which refer to his "youth" or to other philosophers.
12 The classic statement of this doctrine is in Book *Gamma* of the *Metaphysics*.

remaining categories. If intellectual intuition is suppressed, then the essence becomes inaccessible, and we are left with a subject and accidental predicates. This in turn leads to the eventual dissolution of the subject, which also becomes an accidental unity.

Let me emphasize this point. It should be obvious that for Aristotle, the ontological analysis of discourse about separate substances rests upon the intuition of the subject as the owner of its properties. In our perception of Socrates, each of our physical senses has a determinate set of objects: color, sound, touch, and so on. There is no power of sense-perception that allows us to grasp Socrates as the unity of his properties. The senses act together (*koinê aisthêsis*) to draw our attention to a detached collection of properties. Experience may very well lead us to believe that this collection is an ordered independent unity that we identify as a human being, and more particularly as Socrates. But experience cannot provide us with knowledge of how we accomplish this feat. The moment we in fact recognize that the aforementioned collection is indeed an internally articulated unity, we are exercising noetic intuition. Or so Aristotle would say. The moment this contention becomes implausible, the doctrine of essence or *ousia* is effectively jettisoned and we begin our analysis of the separate object of sense perception from linguistic considerations. The operative question thus shifts from "what is it?" to "how shall we best describe it?" All questions of unity are thus answered by considerations of logical form. Since these are based upon agreement or convention, they sooner or later lose their effectiveness. There is accordingly a debate about how best to talk about things, and the unity of experience dissolves into the perspectivism of impressions, sensations, and competing metaphysical schemata.

Another way to bring out the necessity of noetic intuition is by noting Aristotle's reiterated statement that there is no predication with respect to essence.[13] The essence or species-form is predicated of the subject-owner, but the formal elements of the *eidos* are

---

13 E.g., *A.Po* B, 90b28ff. [Ed.: A similar point is made in *Metaph. Z*, at 1034a6 and 1038a33.]

all at the same ontological level in the sense that no one of them is the owner of the others. For example, in the essence "rational animal," neither term is the owner of the other. We cannot construct the *eidos* by individual acts of predication which are themselves rooted in sense-perception. In this sense, we must discover the *eidos*, not produce it.

Once again, there is a parallel here between Aristotle and Plato, but not a convergence. Whereas Plato says that we "see" the Idea, which is obviously separate from us, Aristotle claims instead that the soul "somehow" becomes the things, although he does not explain what he means by this remark.[14] There is so to speak a zone of silence in both Platonism and Aristotelianism, but in the case of Aristotle, the content of intuition is rendered accessible to the discursive faculty of the soul, as is not the case in Plato. In the course of the tradition, intuition is replaced by perception and language; the ensuing metaphysics of production is Aristotelian, not Platonist. This difference is already visible in Aristotle's suspicion of myth, which is the preferred mode of presentation for Plato of the domain of genesis, and hence too of human nature.

If my preceding remarks are on the right track, I have now stated part of the fundamental difference between Plato and Aristotle with respect to the science of being qua being. If such a science, or its prototype, were to exist for Plato, it would have to be dialectic, and this in a sense that takes the Platonic Ideas as prototypes for the primary *ousia* of Aristotle's *Metaphysics*. But *ousia* in Aristotle is secondary as well as primary. The species-form or essence is actualized only and always in separate substances, which of course exist only through ownership of an *eidos*. Neither can be reduced to the other. So far as I can see, Aristotle must give an account of separate substances or logical subjects if he is to achieve a science of being qua being. But the apprehension of these substances as separate unities and ultimate subjects of predication is via common-sense or the *endoksa* of

14   *De Anima* III, 431b17 and b21ff.

serious persons, and this in turn can be verified only through noetic intuition.

I do not need to repeat here the controversy that flourished within analytical philosophy on how to identify natural kinds and more generally, how to articulate the empirical environment into separate and fixed entities. My main point here is rather that even if there were a discursive and deductive science of separate substances, it would hardly be correct to refer to it as an extension of Platonism. Where Plato and Aristotle coincide is in granting the need for the noetic intuition of form. But intuition presents form to discursive analysis; it cannot itself be explained by discursive analysis. Hence the overwhelming temptation in the history of philosophy to jettison noetic intuition. What Heidegger refers to as the greater "scientific" precision of Aristotle in comparison with Plato makes the former the actual father of so-called "productionist" metaphysics.

However we look at it, and contrary to Heidegger's contention, Aristotle is not a Platonist but, as I have shown, gives rise to a completely different ontology from that of his teacher. The following typical passage, taken from the *Introduction to Metaphysics*, illustrates Heidegger's view that Aristotle is a development of Platonic metaphysics: "*Phusis* becomes *idea* (*paradeigma*); truth becomes correctness. The Logos becomes a proposition, it becomes the place of truth as correctness, the origin of the categories, the fundamental proposition about the possibilities of Being. 'Idea' and 'category' are in the future the two titles under which Western thinking, doing, and estimating existence in its entirety, stands."[15] I myself believe, and have now defended the thesis that this account of the history of philosophy is inadequate for two reasons, however helpful it may otherwise be. The first reason is that it ignores the metaphysical difference between Plato and Aristotle. The second is that Aristotle is more responsible for what Heidegger calls the metaphysics of production than is Plato.

15 *EM*, p. 144/202.

In sum, there is no Platonic equivalent to the science of being qua being. The science of dialectic, if there is such a science, addresses itself to Ideas, and thus corresponds at best to the analysis of essences or species-forms in Aristotle's terminology. What the two thinkers share is a reliance upon a cognitive faculty that cannot be analyzed because it is the presupposition for all analyses. It is therefore correct to say that silence is at the heart of Platonic-Aristotelian metaphysics, but this in itself has nothing to do with production, nor does it alter the fact that when the two thinkers do speak, they move in quite different directions.

We take refuge in production in our attempt to fill the silence with logos, but this effort is doomed to failure. It is easier to sustain the effort on an Aristotelian foundation, but to the extent that we succeed, we move farther away from Plato, and finally, from Aristotle himself. The silent center of metaphysics threatens its discursive superstructure with dissolution. We attempt to meet this threat by filling the silence with words. More precisely, we embark on a journey of three stages. First: we say that the essence is invisible, then, unknowable, and finally, non-existent. But this path leads directly to nihilism. Hence we modify our trajectory in one of two ways. Either we become nominalists and stipulate essence to the extent that is required for logical deduction. In other words, essence is redefined as syntax. Or else we attempt to approximate to the invisible essence by an endless series of phenomenological descriptions of how it looks to us. But a pure syntax is talk about nothing, and it is hard to know how to verify phenomenological descriptions of the indescribable. For an essence is not a describable look but the unity of differences that presents itself as a describable look. In one last formulation, the description of a look is not the description of the essentiality of its structure.

In the same period during which Heidegger was developing his interpretation of Platonic metaphysics as productionism, he also propounded the thesis that the Platonist (and so western European) doctrine of Being is a general or "average" conception of what is common to beings of different types.[16] But this accusation can be sustained neither against the Platonic Idea nor the Aristotelian *ousia*.[17] As it happens, it is not difficult to show that Heidegger's generalized view of the Greek conception of Being is erroneous. The being of each kind of particular is not homogeneous with the being of any other kind. To be a cow is quite different from being a horse, and if we add artificial beings to the discussion, both the way of being a cow and a horse are different from the way of being a bed. This is crucial: the Idea or form of a horse exhibits, not simply the being, but the *way* of being a horse. And ways of being are not general.   Heidegger would have to reply that all Ideas or forms have themselves a general structure or nature that is common to all ways of being. This is what Aristotle seems to mean by "being qua being," but as we have just seen, there is no such science in Plato, and the Aristotelian science is one of two quite different but equally necessary senses of *ousia*. Furthermore, just as in the case of the Platonic Ideas, each species-form exhibits a way of being, not just the general or average property of being. If we were to abstract from the particularity of the way of being in each case, we would dissolve the *ousia* in both of its senses as this particular thing of such-and-such a kind. The general characteristics would thus no longer apply to *ousia*. But this is just to say that the resulting ontology would not be Aristotelian. It might perhaps be superior to Aristotle's ontology, but that is no excuse for misrepresenting what Aristotle actually says.

Let me now summarize the consequences of Aristotle's conception of the pre-predicative structure of the essence or species-form. A separate substance is the owner of its properties. It certainly looks as if one of those properties is a species-form of such and such a kind (after all, the *eidos* or species-form is the first in the list of categories). Furthermore, one could argue that it is perfectly possible to analyze essences into their separate components.

16   Cf. *GPP*, 30/22 and *SZ*, 3/22.
17   For further discussion, see Boutot, 50ff.

To take an example, "rational" and "animal," it might be held, are the properties of the essence "human animal." In fact, however, this is a case of synonymy, not predication; the expression "rational animal" is the same as "human animal," because all humans, and only humans, are rational. So "rational" is identical with "human." Otherwise put, "rational" differentiates the genus "animal," but it is not an essential property of the genus because it is normally false to say that "animals are rational." This is enough to show that we cannot know what a human animal is, unless we know what it is to be rational.

It is persons like Socrates who are called "rational animal," not the genus "animal" or the species-form "human being." But we cannot arrive at "rational animal" by predicating one property of an owner. The owner is in this case the unity "rational animal," and not, say, "animal" with the property of rationality. The latter combination would yield the previously rejected "animals are rational." In sum, we can analyze an essence that we already know, but not into the constituents "owner and property." No one part of the essence "stands beneath" or is "thrown" or "built" beneath the others to serve as their support. Sentences describing essences are so to speak phenomenological descriptions rather than predicative propositions. And the forms of phenomenological description are given to cognition, not constructed by it.

It follows that the science of being qua being is not the science of Being in its highest sense (*ousia* as species-form or essence). If there were such a science in Plato, of course, it would be dialectic, that is, the science of the Platonic Ideas. It is therefore a fundamental mistake to assimilate Plato into Aristotle, that is, to treat the doctrine of Ideas as a primitive version of Aristotle's doctrine of being qua being. But neither is the Platonic Idea a primitive version of the Aristotelian *ousia*, since the latter term can serve to designate the *sunolon* or material substance, whereas the Platonic Idea refers exclusively to the intelligible form.

To conclude, without wishing to deny the obvious fact that Aristotle often revises crucial Platonic terms and concepts, I have argued today that the revisions are a sign of the radical split between Plato and Aristotle, not of the existence of a common doctrine called "Platonism." There are (at least) two branches to the tree of metaphysics, and we fall from both these branches, if in fact we do not cut down the entire tree, by insisting upon their underlying unity. Next time I shall take up Heidegger's interpretation of productionism as based upon the discussion of the Idea of the bed in Book Ten of the *Republic*. As a transitional remark, I note that there is no Aristotelian model or version of what Heidegger calls thinking about Being, but there is room for such speculation within Plato, precisely because Plato has no doctrine of being qua being.

Lecture Two:
The Idea of the Bed

Let me begin with a general remark. Heidegger's treatment of Plato and Aristotle, and of their role in the history of metaphysics, is by no means homogeneous. In his Nietzsche lectures, for example, he asserts that Aristotle attempts to return to the pre-Platonic conception of Being. But in the same general context, he continues to stress the underlying unity of the Platonist and Aristotelian metaphysics.[1] In the case of Plato, there is considerable variation in Heidegger's interpretation from one period of his development to another. So too there are occasional remarks that seem to contradict the monolithic application of the doctrine of productionist metaphysics, a doctrine that is one of the central pillars of Heidegger's understanding of Plato.

In this lecture, I am concerned with the central pillar. I shall address the Heideggerian thesis that Plato adopts the paradigm of the demiurge as the dominant element in his doctrine of Ideas, and hence of Being. This thesis receives its characteristic treatment in Heidegger's interpretation of the discussion of Ideas of artifacts in Book Ten of the *Republic*. I want to defend the counter-thesis that Heidegger ignores the political context of this discussion, and at least for that reason, fails to ask himself why Socrates introduces Ideas of artifacts at this point, a thesis that occurs nowhere else in

---

1   N, II, 220–28/159–172. [Ed. Note: The specific remark about Aristotle appears at N, II, 228/171]

Plato, and which Aristotle denies is held by the proponents of the Ideas.[2] Heidegger argues as though the thesis of Ideas in general is easily and typically represented by the account of the Idea of the bed. This is equivalent to taking the carpenter in Book Ten as a metaphor for the philosopher. I shall deny this, but I want also to show that the Socratic analysis, even though motivated by political considerations, points us toward a profound improvement in the standard account of the Ideas.

Palin eks archês. According to Heidegger, European philosophy from Plato to Nietzsche is controlled by the metaphysics of production, that is to say, of Being as *Hergestelltheit*.[3] In my opinion, the actual situation is the reverse. Precisely if we take seriously the account of the Idea of the bed in Book Ten of the *Republic*, we find that Plato clearly distinguishes natural growth from all human constructive activities. Not only this, but he distinguishes the productive activity of the carpenter from mimetic reproduction. The result is a separation, not a continuity, of *phusis* and *technê*. Heidegger himself discusses this distinction at some length in his essay on Aristotle's *Physics*, but for reasons of his own, he in effect denies that distinction to the author of the *Republic*.[4]

There is a second important point in the Socratic analysis. The

---

2   *Metaph.* XIII, 5: 1080a5–6. My thanks to Michael Shaw of Villanova University for reminding me of this passage.

3   *GPP*, 163/116: "Herstellungsunbedürftiges kann überhaupt nur innerhalb des Seinsverständnisses des Herstellens verstanden und entdeckt werden." [Ed.: "What is not in need of Being produced can really be understood and discovered only within the understanding of being that goes with production."] Heidegger finds this "Platonist" thesis throughout the history of ancient and medieval ontologies through to Kant, whose view he summarizes as follows: "Im *Herstellen* von etwas liegt der primäre und direkte Bezug zum Sein eines Seienden. Und darin liegt: *Sein eines Seienden* bedeutet nichts anderes als *Hergestelltheit*" (*GPP*, 213/150). [Ed.: "The primary and direct reference to the Being of a being lies in the production of it. And this implies that "Being of a being" means nothing but producedness."] Heidegger's most extensive discussion of the Idea of the bed occurs in *N I*, 198–217/I, 171–187. See also my previous analysis of this topic in *QB*, 10–21.

4   See "Vom Wesen und Begriff der Φύσις" in , e.g. 359/220–221, 366/226ff.

carpenter is said to "look toward the Idea of the bed" (*pros tên idean blepôn*: 596b7) as the condition of demiurgic production, but he is never said to imitate it. The faculty of imitation is reserved for the painter and poet. The carpenter must therefore acquire knowledge of the nature of beds by a form of vision that reveals what it is to be a bed as the power of imitation does not. Epistemic "looking toward" is not looking at an original model which one then copies. If the wooden bed were an imitation of the Idea of the bed, then Socrates would have contradicted the distinction between knowledge and imitation. Even worse, the Idea of the bed would look like a bed, albeit one that is uniquely perfect, and we would fall into the third-man regress, or more broadly, into the paradoxes of originals and images.

I turn next to the political context. The immediate reason for the introduction of the thesis of Ideas of artifacts is to facilitate the distinction of the crafts, which are necessary for the city, from the mimetic arts, and in particular from mimetic poetry, which must be expelled in order to preserve the existence of the just city.[5] The ostensible license for this expulsion is that poets and painters produce illusions of knowledge that challenge the authority of the philosopher-kings (X. 595a1–b7). The most important example of this production is that of the Olympian gods: hence the ancient quarrel between philosophy and poetry. But at a humbler level, it is equally true that no one can reasonably accuse the bed-maker of knowing nothing about beds, whereas such an accusation is not unreasonable with respect to painters and poets.

The argument begins from the assumption that the craftsman possesses a certain knowledge that is demonstrated by the production of artifacts. Stated succinctly, we can use the wooden bed in order to fulfill the intention implicit in what it is to be a bed. It is also important to note that whereas beds are not natural, their use or function, namely, to allow repose, conforms to our natural need

---

5   For the sake of simplicity, I shall refer to activities like painting and poetry, which we call the "creative" arts, as the mimetic arts, and to the manufacture of objects like beds and tables, as craftsmanship or demiurgy.

for resting, reclining, sleeping, and so on. We could perform these acts without beds, but with great discomfort and lack of security. It is therefore reasonable to say that carpentry or bed-making is a natural element of political life. This was already indicated in Book Two of the *Republic* by Glaucon, who refuses to live in a city of pigs that lacks couches for reclining at meals. On the other hand, it is immediately obvious that we cannot recline or sleep on paintings of beds or poetic descriptions of them. Therefore they are not needed in a healthy city. In fact, Socrates draws a stronger inference. The mimetic arts are politically dangerous because they attempt to mislead us into taking images or illusions for the truth. Accordingly, Socrates expels them from the city.

It should also be kept in mind from the outset that since the carpenter's bed is not a copy of the Idea of the bed, whereas the mimetic artists copy the wooden bed, the Idea cannot be directly accessible to the imitator from the artifact. A portrait of a bed is not a portrait of the Idea of the bed.

The distinction between mimetic and non-mimetic production does not, however, refute Heidegger's thesis of the metaphysics of production. In order to challenge the thesis, we must focus our attention upon a fact that initially supports it. I refer to the fact that there are two kinds of production in the *Republic*, one divine and the other demiurgic. Early in Book Ten, Socrates refers to a god who made the naturally existing bed, in other words, the Idea. This god is identified as a gardener (*phutourgos*: 597d5); Ideas of artifacts are grown or emerge into the light. It is obvious that beds and other man-made artifacts do not grow by nature but are put together or produced. But conversely, the natural bed is not produced out of wood and nails. The poetical language points to a clear difference between divine growth and human production. By nature, growth precedes production and it works with different materials. It would therefore be better to reverse Heidegger's formulation and say that human production is conceived in accord with the model of a divine gardener. I underline this result: neither the craftsman nor the imitator is the paradigm for the production of Ideas.

Let us now look more closely at the producing deity. Socrates says that god wanted to be the genuine maker of the genuine bed, and therefore grew just one that exists in nature (597b5–6), to which the carpenter must look in producing an artifactual bed. This clearly means that god first conceived of the genuine bed and then grew it in the garden of Ideas. Even for the god, discovery precedes production. But the pivotal question here is not why the god wanted to make a unique bed. It is rather why he wanted to make the Idea of the bed at all. No one, not even a god, can conceive of the bed except by first having reflected upon the nature of human beings (and perhaps of gods as well) and their need for repose. This is very important: god looks at the human being and grows (i.e., produces) a divine bed that is itself neither a copy of a human being nor a prototypical bed that can itself be copied by human beings. But the Idea is grown for the sake of human life. And this would of course be true of all artificial Ideas. It would not, however, be true of Ideas of natural kinds, relations, geometrical objects, and so on. This leads us to suspect that the divine gardener is part of the *ad hoc* or political introduction of Ideas of artifacts, rather than a central element in Platonist ontology. I will come back to this point shortly.

In my opinion, we have now taken an important step toward refuting the thesis of a Platonist metaphysics of production. In the Socratic analysis of production, nature, as personified in the divine gardener, grows the Idea of the bed. This lies entirely beyond the capacity of human beings. The activity of craftsmen is not natural growth but artificial manufacture. Such manufacture contains an element of knowledge that Socrates denies to the imitator. One could say that the craftsman imitates the divine gardener in discovering the function of a bed. But the god imitates no one; instead, he discovers what it is to be a bed. Not only does the image of the gardener unite the existence of the Idea of an artifact with the process of nature, whether in the sense of growth or emergence. It also separates the carpenter, painter, and poet – in other words, *technê* – from nature, rather than uniting the two, as Heidegger claims.

To continue with our analysis of the political context, the principal cause of the quarrel between philosophy and poetry is that the poets, by making false copies and so pretending to know the originals, seduce us through the charms of illusion into disobeying the philosopher-kings. By replacing truth with illusion, the poets introduce diversity into the city, since each poet is free to produce his own illusion. The unity of truth is dissolved by a multiplicity of opinions. It is a premise of the political argument that diversity is ugly, whereas unity is beautiful. In this case, beauty and truth coincide, and Socrates asserts that we must unify the city as much as possible. This unity is a desideratum not merely for the bodies of the guardians, but for their souls as well. With respect to the body, unity is served by the abolition of the family, the community of women and children, and the virtually complete absence of privacy and private property. The counterpart in the case of the souls of the guardians is the strict censorship of poetry and the complete suppression of philosophical disagreement. Since the Ideas are the same for everyone, and knowledge is of the Ideas, the foundation is laid for theoretical unity. On this point, there is no difference in the treatment of philosophers and poets in the just city. They share the same disease, namely, the human tendency to diversity, and therefore they require the same medicine.

In order to justify the unity of philosophical doctrine, Socrates must contend that the official teaching of the city is grounded in perfect knowledge of the Ideas, and so that any deviation from it would be a change for the worse. Socrates takes it for granted that the successful production of a bed by the carpenter is a sufficient verification that he knows what it is to be a bed. He does not take for granted, and never suggests, that the carpenter knows what it is to be the Idea of a bed, as the divine gardener presumably does know. The situation with Ideas of natural kinds is in a way the reverse. We do not ask philosophers to produce cows, nor is it their task to answer the question "what is a cow?" Instead, the philosopher is supposed to know that cows exist because of the Idea of the cow. Let me emphasize this. It is the Idea of the cow that produces, or better, allows for the production of, cows. It is not the cow, and certainly not the philosopher, who produces the Idea of the cow. Very far from its being the case that the demiurge is the model for the philosopher, as Heidegger argues, the epistemic component of demiurgy is modeled after the vision of pure Ideas.

To rephrase my previous point, carpenters do not know that they are preserving the unity of the Idea of the bed in the production of its instances. This has to be explained by the philosopher. There is really no analogy at all between the demiurge and the philosopher, except for the fact that each knows something. The carpenter knows how to make beds, and the philosopher knows the science of dialectic, or the doctrine of Ideas. The one thing that the philosopher knows how to make is the city. I will devote a separate lecture to this point. Here we need only mention that there is a difference between theory on the one hand and practico-production on the other. Theory is neither making, nor is it modeled after making.

In sum, justice depends upon unity, and the unity of the city depends upon the underlying unity of philosophical vision. Imitators are dangerous to this unity because their defining function is not based upon knowledge of the objects they copy, but only upon knowledge of the process of imitation itself. But the greater their skill as imitators, the greater their power to deviate from the true nature of things. Imitation is thus the source of corruption. Accordingly, Socrates arrives at the conclusion that the mimetic artists must be expelled from the city. This conclusion surely cannot be extended to include the demiurges, since a city can exist without poets or painters, but not without artifacts. Fortunately, it will not be necessary to banish demiurges like the carpenter if we can show that they are not imitators. And this is shown by attributing to them a vision of the Idea of the pertinent artifact. Finally, we know that they see the Idea because they can make proper beds, which the poet and painter, in their persona as imitators, cannot.

The political motivation underlying the introduction of Ideas of artifacts does not exclude the presence of theoretical issues in

Book Ten of the *Republic*. Stated generally, the sense of sight is not a satisfactory model for the explanation of the "look" of the *idea* or *eidos*, of a bed. Heidegger rightly emphasizes that these Greek words refer to the act of seeing the "face" or visual aspect of something, and he also notes that none of the senses, including vision, is adequate to the task of grasping Ideas (*Seiendes als Seiendes*).[6] But he does not seem to notice that the entire discussion of the Idea of the bed provides us with a hint as to a needed correction of the visual model.

The Idea of the bed is not itself bed-like. I mean by this that it is not a perfect bed that is partly visible to bed-makers, who therefore copy it in a blurred or incomplete manner. The divine bed cannot be copied, which is why imitators are forced to copy artifacts. The nature of the bed is to be slept upon, and this nature is expressed in an endless array of particular beds. It is present in every bed-like object and yet it looks like no bed whatsoever. There is no physical representation of the capacity of being slept upon, but only of things that possess this nature.

It is on this point that the story of the carpenter assumes a theoretical interest comparable to that of the allegory of the cave, about which I shall speak next time. There can be no doubt that the discussion of the Idea of the bed is politically motivated. Nor is there any question that the demiurge is not a philosopher. But there is a similarity between the two, as I noted earlier, insofar as both possess knowledge through the apprehension of Ideas. This knowledge is theoretical in one case and practico-productive in the other, but knowledge of how to make something, as Socrates maintains, is itself, or itself includes, knowledge of what the artifact is. The wooden bed is thus an artifact of practical cognition. It is like the genuine being or Idea but nevertheless is not that being itself (597a1–7). But the divine bed is not an original of which the wooden bed is a copy, in the way that a portrait is a copy of its model. Therefore, in looking at the Idea of the bed, the carpenter is not looking at a bed-like artifact. The Idea of the bed

6   N II, 224/IV, 167–168.

is not a bed nor does it look like a bed in the sense that physical bodies look like each other. To look at the Idea of the bed is not to look at the bed. The only sense in which the produced bed can be "like" the divine bed is in exhibiting the divine nature or power.

As I noted previously with respect to the divine gardener, the carpenter understands what it is to be a bed by reflecting upon the nature of our need for repose. As natural, the need is not produced but discovered. As a function, it is not imitated but exhibited. In my opinion, the point I have just made about the non-produced-ness of the genuine Idea of the bed can also apply to the orthodox cases of Ideas of non-artifactual entities, relations, and moral virtues. I do not produce the Idea of justice by performing a just act. The Platonic doctrine is exactly the reverse; I identify an act, performed or contemplated, as just by "looking at" the Idea of justice. The look is the condition for the identification; otherwise we would not see anything to identify. And most important of all, there is nothing to see in our noetic look at justice that is analogous to the original of a copy, whether poetic or painted.

In sum, the *Republic* provides Heidegger with two portraits of philosophy as knowledge of the Ideas. One model is based upon the criticism of the poets, to whom the philosophers are contrasted as masters of dialectic, the *technê* of dividing "in accordance with forms" (*kat' eidê*: V. 454a4–9) or reasoning with the Platonic Ideas alone (VI. 510b4–9; 533b1–c5; 534b3–7), namely, the pure apprehension of pure forms as fully visible, unchanging, and existing independently of the cognitive process. It is passages like these that Heidegger uses to support his account of the *parousia* thesis. The second model to which Heidegger appeals is that of the philosopher as demiurge or artisan. Intrinsic to this model, as Heidegger himself expounds it, is the thesis that the Ideas *cannot* be fully present to the eye of the soul, since they are "view-points" of human beings, which come into being and pass away.

This conflation of models thus leads to a contradiction in Heidegger's comprehensive portrait of Platonism. If Heidegger's attribution of the *parousia* thesis to Plato is sound, then the model of the demiurge does not apply to it. Ideas cannot be both eternal and produced. One might be tempted to say that the contradiction is in Plato himself, but this seems to entail that the history of metaphysics bifurcates into two different doctrines, only one of which could be called "Platonism." Strikingly enough, Heidegger does claim in the Nietzsche lectures that Platonism bifurcates from the beginning into two doctrines of Being, pure presence (*reine Anwesenheit* or *parousia*) and "rendering possible" (*Ermöglichung*), i.e., production.[7] But this does not lead him to reject the monumental foundation of a unified "Platonism."[8]

It should perhaps be mentioned that the critique of mimesis can be extended from eidetic vision to sense perception. In seeing a physical object, we do not imitate it. One could say that from a neurophysiological standpoint, we construct the object of vision as it is perceived in everyday life. But it is precisely with everyday perception that Socrates begins. And the "look" of the phenomenal cow is not a random concatenation of sensations but owes its particular appearance to the neurophysiological operations themselves, which no one would suggest that we ourselves have constructed.

In any case, the doctrine of Ideas is an attempt to explain the unity and stability of the order of everyday experience, not the laws of optics. Furthermore, the particular "look" or kind of object produced by neurophysiological mechanisms of such-and-such a sort is not an imitation of those mechanisms. Just as I do not manufacture a cow by seeing the Idea of the cow, so too I do not grasp the Idea of a cow by analyzing the effect of the impingement of light rays on the optic nerve or the associated firing of synapses in the central nervous system.

But this is in passing. I have now sketched in broad outline my understanding of the issue of Ideas of artifacts. The craftsman

7   N II, 229/IV, 173.
8   Ibid: "Das Sein ist als das Sichtsame Anwesenheit, aber zugleich das, was der Mensch sich zu Gesicht bringt." [Ed.: "As the visual, Being is presence, but at the same time, what man brings before his eyes."]

knows what a bed is because he knows what it is to safeguard sleep. In looking at the Idea, it is not a bed that he sees, but the power or function that is fulfilled by the production of what we call beds. The manufactured bed is like the Idea in the sense that it is the manifestation of the function. But it is not like the Idea if "like" means here "image of a particular bed." Socrates is therefore right not to apply the term *mimêtês* to the carpenter.

This has an important consequence for Heidegger's general interpretation. He is mistaken to say that the Idea of the bed is available in its copies as well, a mistake that invalidates his assimilation of *technê* and *poiêsis* into *phusis*.[9] The accessibility of the Idea is based upon knowledge of the Idea itself, not on knowledge of how to produce a copy of the Idea. Otherwise put, a painting of a manufactured bed does not transmit the knowledge of the function of beds that underlies the carpenter's capacity to make beds. The proof of the pudding is in the eating. The proof of the bed is in the sleeping. We validate professed knowledge of how to make something by determining whether it fulfils its function, not by looking at it (although sometimes a look suffices to tell us whether the function can be fulfilled).

There is, then, something in the allegory of the carpenter that helps us to understand the doctrine of the Ideas. The account suggests how seeing can be something other than seeing an object suitable for being photographed or painted. In short, the bed produced by the carpenter looks like, in the sense that it reminds us of but is not, the bed produced by a god. And the divine bed does not look like, and is not, the produced bed. A wooden bed is not a copy of the function of a bed. If the divine bed did look like the wooden bed, the third-man paradox would result.

The analysis culminates in the recognition that being and not-being are both to be found in the Platonic Idea. The genuineness or fullness of the being of the Idea of the bed (the facilitation of repose) is inseparable from its not being like the manufactured bed that alone exhibits what it is to be a bed. There is a zone of non-

9   For citations and a more extensive discussion of this point, see *QB*, 13–21.

being, and so of separation or *absence*, that contradicts Heidegger's interpretation of the *parousia* of being, as well as of its production.

On the other hand, the analysis of the doctrine of Ideas is not at all completely separated from our experience of everyday life. The epistemic superiority of the craftsman to the mimetic artist lies in the fact that one cannot make an artifact, say a bed or a table, without knowing its function or power (*dunamis*). This knowledge is confirmed by the utility of the product. X is a bed if and only if we can sleep on it. And this can be determined empirically, without any ontological puzzles. In this way, the craftsman or *technitês* is a common-sense anticipation of the philosopher. But contrary to Heidegger's view, the heart of the anticipation lies in the subordination of production to noetic intuition. Once more: what we intuit is not a picture but a function or power.

In that light we can say that there is no imitation by the carpenter of the "Idea" of the bed, but that the nature of a bed follows from its intended use. What the carpenter looks at in making the bed is not itself a bed. It is a function or formula for existing as a bed, and this in turn is visible in the nature and needs of the human being.[10] Perhaps this is something like what Aristotle means when he says that the soul is the form of artifacts. The function or *dunamis* is not, however, a concept, which is better understood as a discursive or iconic representation of the *dunamis*. In other words, the concept is an epistemic construction that is neither a bed nor the Idea of the bed but an interpretation of the bed. The "Idea" that the carpenter apprehends arises from the unification of factors characterizing the nature of human repose, which factors he does not invent or produce but rather

---

10   This use of power is to be found in *Sph.* 247d8–e4. *Dunamis* receives a somewhat different definition in *R.* 477c1ff, as a genus of beings by which we are able to do what we can do. The step from the latter to the former is not impossible. My point is not that *dunamis* is synonymous with *idea* throughout the dialogues, but that it provides us with a better approach to the Ideas and also repairs the static ocular model in a way that relates the conception of *idea* to that of *phusis*.

discovers. The sight of the Idea is thus not an interpretation in the sense that it could be replaced by something quite different. It mediates between the Idea of the bed, namely, the formula of the elements of repose, and the production of the actual bed. A concept is rather a surrogate for faulty noetic intuition.

Otherwise stated, conceptual discourse about beds is a necessary supplement to the process of constructing them, just as it is to the act by which we apprehend a Platonic Idea. Without such discourse, there would be no knowledge. We have to say something like "the following formula is the Idea of X" and then give the formula or some approximation to it. Without this, all talk of the vision of Ideas is empty. Of course, we can turn emptiness into a virtue by admitting that there is nothing to be said of the inner structure of the Idea, which we simply see noetically as intrinsic to the being of its instances or copies. But this is one of those cases in which vice is superior to virtue.

We have now seen at some length that mimesis is for Socrates opposed to philosophy. Poets are said to imitate the soul or human actions, just as painters imitate bodies. In other words, the craftsman is closer to philosophy than the poet or painter, and he has the added virtue of not expressing political or moral opinions in carrying out his craft.

The genuine knowledge possessed by craftsmen is that of the purpose and practical efficacy of the manufactured objects of their craft. This is something like the dialectician's ostensible knowledge of the Ideas of natural or non-produced entities. But it is not the same. As we have just seen, to know the function of a bed is not to know the ontological structure of the Idea of the bed. The craftsman is thus a defective representation of the dialectician, but to the extent that his activity depends upon intellectual vision of a quasi-noetic sort, he provides us with a standard by which to attack poetry and the fine arts.

Although Socrates does not say so, it seems to follow that the carpenter, who "looks to" but does not imitate the original or ideal bed, is much better suited to rule the city than the poets or painters would be. In other words, the artisan should be at least an adjunct of the philosopher because he produces in the light of the truth. This is in a certain sense implied by the high status given by Socrates to technical knowledge, not only here but throughout the dialogues. The implication, however, must be modified. Whereas craftsmen exercise their proper function in producing good tables and beds, painters and poets do not. Their proper function is to exhibit the many conflicting states of the human soul, and Socrates cites the poets and musicians to this purpose throughout the *Republic*, despite his criticism of their theological and moral deficiencies. The question thus arises: is philosophy like poetry or craftsmanship? With all due respect to carpentry, there is something wrong-headed about Socrates' ranking of these activities. No sane person would turn over the rule of the city to the art of carpentry, but it would be possible to let the poets govern, and one could even suggest, with Shelley, that poets are the unacknowledged legislators of society. This is precisely why Socrates wishes to exclude them from the just city. Carpenters, on the other hand, are concerned with the comfort of the human body.

It is a striking feature of the allegory of the carpenter that its suggestiveness is entirely independent of whether there really are Ideas of artifacts. And there are good reasons to doubt that such Ideas exist. One of the most important of these is that there are endless possible artifacts that do not yet exist. In this case, Ideas would be potential as well as actual. But Socrates always argues that Ideas correspond to existing entities. This is entailed by the "one- over-many" paradigm. To repeat, Socrates says that "we are accustomed to set down some one particular form for each of the particular 'manys' to which we apply the same name" (596a6–7: Bloom translation). This clearly means that Ideas correspond to currently existing particulars. One might argue that Ideas are discovered as our acquaintance with the variety of natural beings expands, but here too the Ideas are actual. It is our knowledge of the Idea, not the Idea itself, that is potential. A potential Idea is ruled out because it could not be genuine and full being. Its very existence would depend upon human praxis; Ideas would be creations, not independent entities. This is precisely Heidegger's claim, but it cannot be substantiated on Platonic grounds. Finally, there is no conceivable limit to the number of possible artifacts. To promote these possibilities to the status of Ideas would paradoxically be to dissolve their illuminative capacity by generating an infinity of intelligible elements; accordingly, the intelligibility of the whole would disappear, and with it, the very notions of wholeness and unity.

Furthermore, it is impossible to describe a potential unity of non-existent objects of which we are not aware. We could of course say that whenever a new artifact is invented, the principle of a one-over-many comes into play. In this case, however, the one in question, namely, the "Idea" of the new invention, is not only produced by human imagination but is subject to modifications of the invention by subsequent technical progress. Ideas of artifacts would thus be in constant flux.

If we allow for non-existent or non-actualized Ideas, how can we exclude imaginary Ideas, and even those whose existence is impossible? Finally, non-existent particulars of a non-existent Idea cannot stand to the latter as images to an original. The only way we can talk about a non-existent Idea is by imagining it as the unity of a class of non-existent particulars. In addition, not yet discovered Ideas are clearly not perspectives or subjective viewpoints onto anything at all. As for Ideas of actually existing artifacts, their radical difference from all humanly produced instances is clear from the fact that they are said by Socrates to originate in the work of nature, which is represented here as a god, whether a carpenter or a gardener (597b6–c3, d1–3; 597d5).

The natural status of the original productive act is repeated several times by Socrates in this passage (597d3, d5, d7, e4, e7, 598a1). A gardener, for example, does not produce a plant *ex nihilo* but uses natural elements such as seeds and pollen as well as soil, fertilizer, and water. We must therefore distinguish between the growth of Ideas through the work of divine nature, and the production of copies of these Ideas by human cognition. Natural growth is a metaphor for the contribution of intelligibility and being by the Good to the independent Idea that is not produced but reproduced in those artifacts.

Whether or not Socrates is serious in attributing natural growth to the work of a god, it is quite clear that he means to rule out the possibility that the Ideas are produced by human beings. There is however a definite flavor here, represented by the image of god as gardener, of what Heidegger himself refers to as the original sense of *phusis* as sprouting or emerging into the sunlight, like plants. The connection between *phusis and dunamis* leaves room for a dynamic interpretation of Being that is nevertheless not "productionist" in Heidegger's sense of the term, but is reminiscent of the Eleatic Stranger's appeal to *dunamis* in the *Sophist*.[11] The immediate reference to the Idea of the bed is unexpected in this context; since beds do not grow, a carpenter-god would be more appropriate at this point than a divine gardener.

In either case, Socrates' language certainly implies that the god made the Idea of the bed consciously if not intentionally. At 597c1–5, he says that the god was either compelled or wished to make just one bed, "only that very one that is a bed" (*mian monon autên ekeinên ho estin klinê*, a phrase that reminds us of *autê hê klinê*). If this is supposed to be taken literally, it must mean that the divine gardener thinks of the *dunamis* of the bed before growing its *energeia* in his ontological garden. This is consistent with the procedure of the carpenter. A more likely alternative is that Ideas are natural, and so, if they can be said to come into existence at all, it can only be through the spontaneity of nature.

Allow me to restate the most important point of my lecture thus far. Given the orthodox or visual model of the noetic intuition of Ideas, the carpenter's bed both must and yet cannot look like the divine or natural bed. If it looks like the Idea or *dunamis* of the natural bed, this leads to the third-man regress. But if it does not look like the natural bed, the carpenter's bed must look like something other than its Idea, which seems to be a

---

11 See Note 9 above and my *Plato's Sophist* (South Bend, Indiana: St. Augustine's Press, 1999), 219–220. [Ed.: Rosen is referring here to the Stranger's definition of true being (*ontôs einai*) at Sph. 247d8–e4 as "nothing other than power" (*ouk allo ti plên dunamis*)."]

self-contradiction. On this alternative, there is no apparent reason why the carpenter should look at the Idea of the bed for knowledge of how to make a wooden bed, even though the Idea is supposed to be the bed's natural "look." This is to say that the nature of what it is to be a bed does not resemble actual beds. In this case it is impossible to see how a manufactured bed can be an image of the original Idea. We solve the problem by shifting from pictorial originals to *dunameis*.

If it is correct that the Idea of the bed is not a supreme or perfect bed, but rather the function of beds, then we may be said to arrive at the understanding of a bed without seeing a complete manifestation of the fully present form of the bed. We move from the understanding of the function to a visual image of a bed, and not from a quasi-visual intuition of the perfect bed to its produced copy. In so doing, we also free philosophy from mimesis. In slightly different terms, seeing is not enough. We have to understand what we see. But the converse is also true. In order to know something, we must see or come into contact with what it is that we wish to know.

Philosophical knowledge is not mimesis, inasmuch as mere copying is not understanding. But this requires us to supplement radically the visual model of eidetic intuition. Socrates does not explain how this is to be done. That is, he does not explain why looking at the Idea of the bed enables the carpenter to make a bed without becoming an imitator. What he does is to indicate the condition for such an enterprise. The Idea of the bed cannot be taken to look anything like actual beds. It cannot be imitated in the sense of being copied or duplicated in pictures or words.

In the last part of this lecture, I want to consider the inadequacy of Socrates' account of imitation. My point here will be analogous to the main point about Ideas. Just as the grasp of Ideas cannot be adequately explained solely on the model of vision, so too imitation is not reducible to copying, in the sense of producing a replica of an original. One can imitate without producing a copy of a fully visible original.

Socrates' treatment of painting and poetry as forms of mimesis is obviously inadequate on his own terms. It is easy to see that the practitioners of these arts are not interested in beds, but rather in illuminating states of the soul. Despite his criticism of mimesis, Socrates regularly cites Homer and other poets throughout the *Republic* in order to sustain his own analysis of human nature. Furthermore, the dialogues are themselves dramas or poems, but not imitations. Plato does not imitate life in the sense of copying it, as a painter is said to copy the carpenter's bed.

Nor can he be said to copy Ideas. The *Sophist* is no more a portrait of being than is the *Symposium* a portrait of eros. One can copy a manuscript or photograph a painting, but this is not the same as writing a dialogue or painting a portrait. I mean by this that one cannot produce copies of life that are not themselves life. Even the explanation or interpretation of life is itself an aspect of life, and not something external to it but resembling it. The expression "true to life" means that a work of art expresses some truth about life, but the life of the actors in a novel or play is not a copy of the life of those who read the novel or attend a performance of the play.

Allow me to illustrate this general point with a brief survey of three kinds of imitation that do not exhibit the defect attributed by Socrates to the genus. These three are portraying, emulating, and ridiculing.

One kind of portrayal is the portrait by a painter. Socrates speaks of painting as attempted duplication. But this interpretation can scarcely be reconciled with his own example of the bed. No one could mistake a painting of a bed for the bed itself, but this is a secondary point. The main consideration is that painters are accused of possessing defective knowledge of the object they copy, because the copy is a defective version of the original. But the intention of the painter is not to deceive us into taking his painting for a real bed. Socrates settles the issue in advance by attributing an absurd purpose to the painter. We can, however, easily infer from the example of poetry that the intention of the painter is to convey knowledge about the users of beds and not to provide blueprints for their construction.

A second example of portrayal is one that was very familiar to Socrates: the drama. When an actor in a play undertakes to portray an ancient hero, say Odysseus, he is not trying to provide us with a four-dimensional copy of the original, but rather to evoke his presence by an interpretation of what it might be like to be Odysseus. The interpretations of two different actors may differ from each other even as both are successful. And the same considerations apply to poets. Odysseus himself is an example of a pagan hero, all of whom are no more copies of the paradigmatic hero than are wooden beds of the divine paradigm. In short, we could say that a certain actor imitates Odysseus without intending to imply that he wishes to duplicate the hero, like a mimic who repeats everything that we say and do.

To this we should add the striking case of Plato's portrait of Socrates, or rather of a Socrates grown young and beautiful. The portrait is hardly a copy, as Plato's expression makes clear. It is instead an imitation of what it would be like to be a philosopher. One might wish to refer to the portrait as an interpretation rather than an imitation, but this is not quite adequate. Plato intends his portrait of Socrates to reveal the truth about the philosophical nature, not to provide us with one interpretation among many. Perhaps we can say that there are many interpretations of this single truth, and so that we see here a one-over-many. In other words, the "Idea" of the philosopher is imitated in this particular way, and it could be imitated in others, without changing the imitation into an interpretation of a purely subjective kind.

The second kind of mimesis to be considered is what I shall call emulation. I note in passing that a portrait could be produced in order to encourage emulation. The purpose of the Platonic dialogues is presumably to encourage, at least in some of their readers, the desire to emulate Socrates. But this is not necessary. We can be instructed by an account of the life of Oedipus without wishing to emulate it. A good example of art for the sake of emulation is a play or poem about a hero that encourages us to perform brave acts for the sake of the mother-land. It hardly needs emphasizing that to imitate a brave act is not to paint its portrait, although in certain circumstances, the painting of such a portrait might itself be a brave act.

Someone who is inspired to act bravely through the example of another is not attempting to deceive us about the nature of his own act, nor is the inspired act a false or imperfect version of the original. On the contrary, it is a new act, similar to its predecessor only in belonging to the same "many" or collection of brave acts. In other words, just as in the case of poems and paintings, brave acts constitute a legitimate example of a one-over-many, and so fulfil the Socratic criterion for an Idea.

There is more that could be said about emulation, but I turn instead to the third kind of imitation. Whether on the stage or in certain circumstances of actual life, one person may mimic another's words and deeds in a way that seems to come the closest of our three kinds to Socrates' account of mimesis. Those who observe such performances, as for example in comedies, are nevertheless under no illusion that the mimic is attempting to persuade us that he is himself the person he mimics. On the contrary, the usual reason for such a performance is to ridicule the person mimicked. At the heart of this ridicule is the desire to convey something about the character or actions of the given person. The audience is to be instructed through laughter.

This is as far as we need to go in our discussion of mimesis. We can explain the weakness of the account of mimesis in the *Republic* as due to the political program of Socrates. This political program, however, has certain unfortunate consequences for what we can call the "theoretical" dimension of Platonism. One consequence is to provide some credence for the assertion that Plato is not entirely free of a metaphysics of production. In preserving the craftsman from expulsion, Socrates associates him with the philosopher, thereby partially obscuring the difference between philosophy and demiurgy.

So far as Plato's intentions are concerned, it seems undeniable that he wished to preclude such a metaphysics. Stated as concisely as possible, the metaphysics of production entails the dissolution of the difference between philosophy and poetry. More precisely, philosophy turns into poetry. The natural order is replaced by a historical sequence of poems. What we can then call the "being" or the mode of presentation of the being of poetry is history. We cannot rank-order the historical sequence of poems because all standards for such an ordering are themselves poems. Even the edifying invocation to escape the nihilism of poetry is itself a poem. And perhaps worst of all, the origin of poetical thinking or discourse is not discourse but silence.

What is the decisive answer of the Platonist to this sequence of events? There is only one candidate for this crucial role: the doctrine of Ideas. To this extent, Heidegger is justified in concentrating his analysis of Platonism on the problem of the Ideas. But Plato does not provide us with a canonical text that supplies us with a detailed account of the doctrine of Ideas. The discussion in Book Ten of the *Republic* is especially vexing because it goes contrary to what is regularly stated in the other dialogues, and even in other parts of the *Republic*. And it presents such important issues as mimesis and the one-over-many schema with an apparent carelessness and lack of sound reasoning that is due to the political program, not to the exigencies of metaphysical or ontological thinking. I have tried to take into account the political context in addressing the theoretical difficulties in the discussion of the Idea of the bed. At the heart of these difficulties is the nature of mimesis.

In the first and longest part of my lecture, I showed how one could sustain the difference between looking to an Idea and imitating an artifact. This was necessary since the artifact itself, e.g., the bed, is available for imitation only because it has been produced by the carpenter. Socrates must therefore show that the initial act of production is not an imitation. In the second part of my paper, I argued that it is necessary to expand Socrates' treatment of mimesis in a way analogous to an expansion of the doctrine of Ideas.

Let me add a final word about the schema of the one-over-many. As it stands, the schema may be employed to identify Ideas of artifacts as well as of natural entities, and in fact, Socrates applies it to the case of the bed. This opens the door to potential and imaginary Ideas, and thus leads, not to a modification of Platonism but to its suppression. It has to be shown that the schema, if it is to be retained, must apply to natural kinds only. In the language of the *Republic*, the production of Ideas cannot be attributed to human beings, but only to a god who is not a carpenter but a gardener. Unfortunately, Socrates says nothing in the tenth book of the *Republic* that casts any light on how to restrict the scope of his "customary procedure" to natural kinds. To do so would be to destroy the point about the political correctness of demiurgy.

Lecture Three:
Parousia

One of the claims most frequently repeated by Heidegger is that Plato understands Being as *parousia* or presence.[1] Heidegger is of course himself fascinated with notions of unconcealment, coming into the light, and openness. But the view attributed to Plato is not the same as that of Heidegger himself. According to Heidegger, Plato takes his bearings by that which is presented, whereas he himself refers primarily to the horizon of presentation. On the Heideggerian account, Platonism both overlooks the temporality of presence and obscures the fundamental process of opening and lighting-up that is the necessary precondition for the visibility of any present entity. This shift in attention from presentation to presence leads us to identify what is present through its attributes (*etwas als etwas*) rather than through its Being.

A further consequence in Heidegger's interpretation is that Plato is said to shift from the original Greek understanding of the truth of Being as dependent upon unconcealment, to a conception of truth as a correspondence between what is disclosed and how it looks to us. Not only is Being concealed by beings, but these latter submit to the measure of human perspective. This is the origin

---

1   For a detailed examination of this point, see Alain Boutot, *Heidegger et Platon* , 53–64. For a concise statement by Heidegger of the shift in Greek thought from *phusis* to *parousia*, see *EM*, 46–48/64–66. There is a long discussion of *parousia* in Plato in *WMF*, 51/36ff.

of the thesis that truth is a property of a proposition that expresses the aforementioned correspondence of the disclosed look to the
eye of the perceiver. In contemporary parlance, truth is a predicate
or artifact of language, whereas for Heidegger it is a property of
Being. Correlatively, by emphasizing fullness of presence, Plato
loses sight of the process by which Being is actually disclosed or
"torn" from concealment, and so he turns away from the priva-
tive element in that process.

There is more than one reason for initial doubt concerning this
interpretation of Plato. To begin with, it depends heavily upon
etymological analyses of Plato's terminology. This is sometimes
illuminating, but the method has to be employed with extreme
caution. There is no reason to prefer in all cases an original or root
meaning of a technical term that has been redefined in a new
sense. More specifically, if *parousia* means "presence" and Plato
assigns a sense to that term which explicitly excludes the original
temporal sense, there is no reason to claim that the temporal sense
has escaped his attention, or that it takes precedence over the new
definition. Heidegger's bias toward origins reminds one of the
Biblical notion of a pure beginning that is very soon covered over
by the fall of mankind. This motif is also to be discerned in
Nietzsche's conception of genealogy, which plays an important if
often subterranean role in Heidegger and his successors.

Second, it has been suggested (by Boutot) that *parousia* seems
to mean "next to" rather than "to be present."[2] According to
Heidegger, "next to" is the vulgar sense of *parousia*.[3] The least
one can say in reply is that it is rather difficult to separate the concept of something as present to something else from the sense of
being next to in a spatial rather than a temporal sense. When the
spatial sense is explicitly said to be what is intended, it seems arbitrary and unjustified to insist that the temporal sense prevails.
Boutot cites *Phaedo* 100d5, where Socrates speaks of "the *parousia* or *koinônia* of beauty itself, or however we choose to call it."

2   Ibid., 62–63/43–45.
3   *WMF*, 61/43.

The term *koinônia* ("communion") does not have a root sense of temporality. To this observation by Boutot I add that a few lines prior to the passage which he cite from the *Phaedo*, Socrates uses the verb *metechei* or "participates," from which is derived the technical and non-temporal term *metheksis*. In general, one can say that the technical Platonic vocabulary is not always derived from temporal notions, but that even where it is, Plato's *personae* make clear their intention to contrast being with temporality. This intention cannot be refuted any more than it can be established on the basis of etymological analysis. Etymological evidence becomes more persuasive in the context of the Platonic myths, but even there one must ascertain the discursive context of the relevant terms.

I propose to argue, in any case, that Plato's conception of Being as that which is always (*aei on*), requires him to deny, or let us say to qualify very sharply, the thesis of truth as the full presence of what is fully and forever. The best we can do is to achieve a temporary presence of a partial manifestation of the Platonic Idea. But truth is one thing, and Being is another. It will be my contention that Plato associates cognition, not Being, with temporality. Despite all talk of intellectual intuition and the metaphor of the sun, it is entirely unclear how the human intellect could verify the eternal, or for that matter sempiternal duration of an Idea through direct intuitive contact. We can only verify the presence of an Idea for the time during which we perceive it. The step from presence to eternal Being is inferential or discursive, not simply perceptual. As Socrates says in the *Phaedo* 101d2–7), it is a safe hypothesis. In general, we must first reason from the intelligibility of particular things to the necessity of an Idea, nature, or power that is common to each kind of thing. Second, we must demonstrate the eternity of intelligible structure, in some sense of the term *aei* that does not depend upon the perpetual presence of the individual philosopher.

This, I believe, is why all talk of the vision of the Ideas is presented as the result of an upward ascent or culmination of the process by which we analyze the relative stability of the perceptual cosmos. From this standpoint, the movement from particulars to an Idea is analogous to the movement from elements to a set. The most one could say is that in our discursive progress from the particular to the Idea, we are illuminated by the eternal structure of intelligibility. That is, we arrive retrospectively at a "recollection" of the inner structure of class membership, or of what it is to be this thing here of such and such a kind. One can therefore agree with Heidegger that unconcealedness is the precondition of discursive or propositional reasoning, without forgetting that we must reason discursively in order to arrive at an awareness of that precondition.

Finally, it is not in Plato's view the light of reason that illuminates beings, as Heidegger claims, but rather the Idea of the Good (*R.* VI, 508e3–509b6), which in so doing fulfills the function of the Heideggerian *Lichtung* or openness upon which light depends. It is true that Socrates represents this openness with the metaphor of a thing or *on*, namely, the sun. But we cannot see the sky without the light of the sun, moon, and stars.[4]

Heidegger himself seems to fluctuate between visual and auditory metaphors in his own account of Being and truth. But he underplays, or omits altogether, the crucial role of *logos* as the mediation between seeing and hearing. And this weakens the force of his otherwise valuable criticism of the excessive role assigned by Plato to visual metaphors. Heidegger exaggerates the role of the perceptual model in Plato's metaphysics. I offered an extended analysis of this point in my previous lecture. Today I plan to supplement that analysis with a consideration of the problem of *parousia*.

My goal is not to refute Heidegger so much as to show that he shares common ground with Plato. For example, Heidegger's adaptation of Husserlian themes connected with the intentionality of human activity, and in particular of thinking, is also extremely suggestive with respect to the role of perception in Plato's

---

4   See *EP,* 80–85.

epistemology.[5] Husserl argues persuasively that it is possible to intend an object that is not fully or originally present to perception, and that this intention is the basis for full presence or evidence. The shift to evidence is thus the emergence from absence into presence.

In my previous lecture, I showed how one can understand the intuition of an object that is not fully present by studying Socrates' account of the production of artifacts. In this lecture and the next, I am going to present the corollary thesis that Plato portrays truth as suffused with darkness or absence, without repudiating the claim that Being is to be understood as *aei on*, and hence as discovered, not produced.[6] Production takes place within human cognition in order to fill the gap between the partial presence of Being and its fulfillment in wisdom. This obviously has nothing to do with the sound Heideggerian observation that perception plays a central role in Plato's philosophy. My claim is rather that Plato was aware of the difference between full perception and the perception of absence. It is true that Plato presents this difference almost entirely in terms of the metaphor of vision; but in the case of presence and absence, this is entirely appropriate.

Let us begin, as both Plato and Heidegger recommend, with everyday life. It is not a metaphysical proposition, but an observation of common sense, that darkness is the natural correlate of light. In the domain of perception and cognition, and not only there, we normally prefer light to darkness. We speak favorably, for example, of receiving an illumination or seeing what to do, but unfavorably of being cast into the dark. The same points hold good with respect to absence. We notice that something or someone is absent because it or he is not present, as we expected them to be. In general, a partial disclosure is identified as such only by our imaginative projection of complete visibility. And if an object

---

5   For a detailed analysis, see Daniel Dahlstrom, *Heidegger's Concept of Truth* (Cambridge: Cambridge University Press, 2001), especially Chapter 2.

6   See also my paper, "Suspicion, Deception, and Concealment," in *Metaphysics in Ordinary Language* (New Haven and London: Yale University Press 1999), Chapter 1.

is completely absent, we know this only because of the presence of the context from which it makes sense to refer to a lacuna. In this sense, even the perception of passing time has a strong visual component. Most directly, we look at the clock to see how much time has passed. At a deeper level, we experience the passage of time by the changing image of our face in the mirror. And still more fundamentally, our sense of the temporal structure of existence cannot be given an interpretation without recourse to visual metaphors. We cannot, for example, be "on the way" without a spatial orientation that distinguishes our point of departure from its authentic terminus. We must *see* where we are going if we are not to fall into the abyss of the silent voice of conscience.

As this brief survey suggests, there seems to be no reason to object to the priority of presence over absence in the philosophical analysis of everyday life, that is, in our study of the phenomena, although we must grant that there are different modalities of presence, including that of an inferred absence. The situation would be different if we excluded absence and darkness from our epistemological and ontological vocabularies. Indeed, the correlativity of these two terms with presence and light makes such an exclusion impossible. Even if we accept the Heideggerian claim that Being is for Plato what is always, this claim to full presence is intelligible only in contrast to the coming to be and passing away of the generated instances of the Ideas. Full visibility would be equivalent to complete blindness. For this reason, one might expect Plato to provide us with evidence of his awareness of the situation.[7] That is, we would expect him to indicate the continued "presence" of a penumbra of absence or darkness that both makes possible and qualifies our apprehension of a Platonic Idea. I am going to show that this is precisely the case in the very text that Heidegger uses as one of his main supports for the attribution to Plato of a metaphysics of full presence. But let me first restate in a slightly different way Heidegger's interpretation of Platonic

7   See *P*, 186/125, where he says that the myth of Er originates in the *Wesenseinheit* of *Verborgenheit* and *Unverborgenheit*

parousia. I take my bearings by the difference between Heidegger's own emphasis upon light and the role played by light in Plato.

Stated in an introductory manner, the central contention of Heidegger's attack against what he calls Platonism is that its exaggerated preference for light arises from the relatively greater precision of visual in comparison with other types of sense-perception, as noted by Aristotle in the opening lines of the *Metaphysics*.[8] This in turn leads to the connection between visibility and things that can be measured, controlled, and thus put to use. As a consequence, at the metaphysical as well as cognitive and perceptual level, our attention shifts from the process of illumination to the entities that are illuminated. In the crucial instance, Being is concealed by the entities that it manifests, and eventually this concealment is itself concealed.[9] There is an echo here of the Fichtean doctrine of the covering over of the absolute ego by its own finite productions. But such esoteric affiliations are superfluous, since everyday life gives us many examples of our failure to see the forest for the trees.

For Heidegger, then, Plato's emphasis upon vision leads directly to an unnoticed darkening of the visual field. The first stage in this darkening is the conceptualization of the source or ground of Being as an Idea or determinate look, represented metaphorically as the sun and called both the Good and the Idea of the Good. This vacillation in the title reflects an inner confusion in Plato's mind concerning the nature of the Good. In other words, the cause of Being, which is said to be "beyond Being" (*epekeina tês*

8 [Ed.: The reference is to *Metaph.* 980a20–27. According to Aristotle, our fondness for sight is greater by virtue of its making clear many differences (*pollas dêloi diaphoras*) in things.]

9 For an example of this frequently reiterated theme, see *N*, II, 360–63/IV, 219–220. One should also be careful to distinguish between what I call the "being-process" or the properties of Being as it is projected by the flow of time and "die Lichtung des Seins," which refers, not to light but to the openness within which Being comes into the light. According to Heidegger, Plato fails to think of this openness, which is a precondition of *Licht* and so of the Ideas. See note 4 above.

ousias), is itself reified, and its function is explained by analogy with the sun. "Good" comes to mean "useful" or "suitable" (*tauglich*)[10] for seeing other determinate looks, also called Ideas or forms, which can be counted and measured by the art of dialectic. The conceptual grasp of vision thus emancipates the tactile grasp that unleashes the age of technology.

Despite the peculiarity of Heidegger's own terminology, his thesis has been widely influential, especially as it is contained in his interpretation of Nietzsche. Let us say that Heidegger assimilates Nietzsche's psychological attack on Platonic Ideas into the language of ontology. For example, one still hears the dialectic of Apollo and Dionysus in Heidegger's claim that the truth must be captured from the darkness. The following passage, cited from Heidegger's preface to the study by W. J. Richardson, illustrates the role of this dialectic in Heidegger's alternative to the Platonist concealment of Being:

> If we replace "Time" by the lighting of the self-hiding of *Anwesen* (presence as holding itself together and before), then Being defines itself out of the projective scope of Time. But this results only in so far as the lighting of self-hiding puts to its use a thinking that corresponds to it. *Anwesen* (Being) belongs to the lighting of self-hiding (Time). Lighting of self-hiding (Time) produces *Anwesen* (Being).[11]

Allow me to restate this text in somewhat simpler language. Being belongs to time as that which hides within it: as so hiding it

---

10 *PLW*, 225/174.
11 Heidegger's Preface to W. J. Richardson, SJ, *Heidegger: From Phenomenology to Thought* (The Hague, M. Nijhoff: 1963), p. 21. [Ed.: I provide here the German original from Heidegger's letter to Father Richardson: "Setzen wir statt 'Zeit': Lichtung des Sichverbergens von Anwesen, dann bestimmt sich Sein aus dem Entwurfbereich von Zeit. Dies ergibt sich jedoch nur insofern, als die Lichtung des Sichverbergens ein ihm entsprechendes Denken in seinen Brauch nimmt. Anwesen (Sein) gehört in die Lichtung des Sichverbergens (Zeit). Lichtung des Sichverbergens (Zeit) erbringt Anwesen (Sein)."]

presents itself (*es gibt Sein*) as the "way" in which time proceeds. Heidegger does not say that Being *is* time, but that it is accessible as hiding, i.e., as concealed, through a projection onto time, and so as within time. Furthermore, time presents or illuminates this self-hiding; here we see Heidegger's historicism. There are temporal epochs of the presentation or historicity of Being. Accordingly, the Platonist attempt to surpass temporality by attributing eternity to Being leads directly to the *concealment* of self-concealment, and not its illumination. The reification of light is an unconscious surrender to darkness.

The passage just cited shows that Heidegger himself conceives of Being in conjunction with light. But light is for him a process of illumination, a "lighting-up," and so an emergence from darkness, rather than the visibility of *what* is illuminated. One sees here Heidegger's preference for the pre-Socratic or (as he designates it) genuine Greek conception of Being as *phusis*: growth, coming into the light.[12] Heidegger's fundamental critique of Plato is thus directed, not against the connection between light on the one hand and truth and Being on the other, but rather against the turn from the opening of the lighting process to the determinate looks of what is illuminated. Otherwise stated, the aforementioned turn shifts our gaze from what is unveiled by the light, to the act of intellectual vision, or how things can be brought under the control of human intelligence. *Phusis* loses its dimension of growth and thus, implicitly, its subterranean connection with temporality. In slightly different terms, Plato turns away from the dark side of the truth, whereas Heidegger, despite his emphasis upon lighting-up and emergence from darkness, retains the element of hiddenness within the achievement of truth. In a word, Plato initiates the shift from ontology to epistemology.

---

12 Cf. *EM*, 11–12/15–16:
"Die *phusis* ist das Sein selbst, kraft dessen das Seiende erst beobachtbar wird und bleibt . . . *Phusis* ist das *Ent-stehen*, aus dem Verborgenen sich heraus—und dieses so erst in den Stand bringen." [Ed.: "*Phusis* is Being itself, by virtue of which beings first become and remain observable . . . *Phusis* is the event of *standing forth*, arising from the concealed and thus enabling the concealed to take its stand for the first time."]

In his interpretation of the Platonic forms or Ideas, Heidegger resorts to what one might almost call "psychoanalysis." Briefly stated, he holds that the Ideas, which Plato claimed to be the full presence to the eye of the soul of what is fully visible, are in fact the archetypes of the will to power. In other words, they are Nietzschean perspectives.[13] I speak of psychoanalysis here because Plato's presumed error concerning his own doctrine is evidently an unconscious result of cognitive manipulation through what Heidegger would perhaps call the errance of being.[14]

I mentioned previously that according to Heidegger's interpretation, there is an intimate connection between the concealment of Being and the Platonist reversal of the authentic Greek conception of truth. Plato's Ideas distract us from considering the interplay of light and darkness that is conveyed in the Greek word for "truth": *alêtheia*. Heidegger translates this as *Unverborgenheit* and treats the alpha-privative in the Greek word as active: a kind of non-conceptual grasping or wrenching of the truth from its initial concealment. Underlying the notion of concealment is the concept of the temporality through which we have access to Being. In Derrida's criticism of the Platonism of Husserl, for example, the ostensible presence of Being is differentiated or deferred by the acts of remembering and expecting. Presence is in fact representation, and in this sense is always delayed by dependence upon the past and the future. Time is present only as absenting itself.[15]

In sum, according to Heidegger's version of Plato, the doctrine

---

13 This of course does not mean that Plato consciously prefigures Nietzsche; in the *idea* there is no trace of the experience of *Sein* as will to power (*N*, II, 245/IV, 186–187). Plato's metaphysics is hidden nihilism (ibid., 345/IV, 206), i.e., the doctrine of Being as will to power.

14 "Das sich seit Platon das Wirkliche im Lichte von Ideen zeigt, hat nicht Platon gemacht. Der Denker hat nur dem entsprochen, was sich ihm zusprach."*FNT*, 25/18. [Ed.: "The fact that the real has, ever since Plato, been showing itself in the light of Ideas, Plato did not bring about. The thinker only responded to what addressed itself to him."]

15 For a convenient treatment of Derrida's adoption of Heidegger, see his *Speech and Phenomena And Other Essays on Husserl's Theory of Signs* (Evanston, Ill: Northwestern University Press, 1973), 52, 65.

of *parousia* is adopted, not for the sake of pure contemplation, but in order to control the beings of everyday life. This is not a conscious and intentionally hidden plot on Plato's part, but his response to what was spoken to him by Being itself. Heidegger here retains the Hegelian notion of the philosopher as the passive voice of actuality at a given epoch. The voice of Being leads Plato to the production of looks or paradigms to serve as the standards for determining what is useful. Truth is now a property of the cognitive process, not of Being, which is itself redefined as the content of our epistemic constructions.

In other words, Being is reified and also subjectified. It is concealed by the products of this construction. Our conception of Being is redefined with respect to beings. A view or look (*idea* or *eidos*) of something in particular is constructed that is relative to the onlooker and that provides a human standard by which to measure the correctness of our representation of it. And correctness, of course, is a property of the proposition, not of Being.[16] From here, it is a short step to the more technical development of this doctrine by Aristotle, who says in the *Metaphysics* that "the false and the true are not in the things (*pragmasin*) . . . but in *dianoia*."[17] And this underlies the development of the Western tradition of the proposition and of truth as a predicate. Plato is unwillingly subsumed under the crucial axiom of modern philosophy that we know only what we make. In seeing the Ideas, the eye of the soul sees itself. What looks like the presence of something other than the soul is an optical illusion.

As a transition to the next section of my lecture, which is devoted to Platonic exegesis, I want to make three brief remarks. The first is that the entire Heideggerian interpretation of *parousia* in Plato is based upon the doctrine of Ideas. Not even in his famous interpretation of the allegory of the cave, which we are going to study with some care, does Heidegger focus upon the human soul and its erotic nature. As I am about to show,

16   *PLW*, 224–228/173–177.
17   *Metaph.* E4, 1027b2527.

however, the hypothesis of the Ideas cannot by itself provide us with an account of Being and truth.

In slightly different terms, the question "what is Being" is for Heidegger dependent upon our answer to the antecedent question "who is *Dasein*?" But this is an ontologized version of the Socratic question "who am I?" From a Socratic standpoint, Heidegger begs the question of human nature by beginning with his fundamental ontology as the correct theoretical method for explicating the phenomena. In other words, the phenomena themselves appear through the screen of phenomenology. Plato tries to avoid methodological circularity by beginning with the drama of everyday life. It is not at all self-evident that a theoretically neutral beginning is possible, but it seems obvious that the question "who am I?" is closer to the origins than the question "Who is *Dasein*?" To this I add that Heidegger never licenses us to ask "who is Being?" because the question would be absurd. But its absurdity radically weakens his attack upon Plato's doctrine of Ideas.

Second, I remind you that Heidegger replaces the ontology of presence by a doctrine that gives equal if not greater importance to absence. That which appears or presents itself does so within the structure of human temporality, and so as either about to disappear or not yet to have arrived. The temporal present is continuously dissolving into the past and coming to be the future. What is ontologically present is, as it were, not the temporal present but the ecstatic circle of the three dimensions of temporality.[18] Since Being is accessible to us only through time, the fullness of presence attributed to the Platonic Idea is impossible. What is actually present is the dynamic of absence, whether as dissolved into the past or as not yet having emerged from the future. I use the term "dynamic" to express Heidegger's virtual identification of presence with possibility.[19] For Heidegger, actuality is a transient residue of possibility: "Possibility is higher than actuality."[20]

18   SZ,329/377, 350/401.
19   This is not entirely satisfactory, since *Möglichkeit* does not mean *Macht* or *Kraft*, whereas *dunamis* can be translated as "power."
20   SZ, 38/63.

Despite the praise of unconcealment, absence and darkness, in the form of temporality and human finitude, acquire a priority over presence and light.

Third: whereas Heidegger is in a real sense a philosopher of language, he is not centrally concerned with reading or writing, and so not with seeing. I mean by this that for him, what we see is the lighting process, not a *Ding, pragma*, or *on*. In the case of Being, the operative metaphor is frequently that of hearing. I have sometimes observed playfully that Heidegger is a Jew who is forbidden to look upon the face of God but must seek instead to hear his speech. I note that we can hear in the dark, but not read or see. On the other hand, the voice of God utters commandments, which can be carved in stone and inscribed on parchment, whereas the voice of Being is silent. Stated succinctly, Heidegger preserves the atmosphere of revealed religion, but without any access to God, that is, to the *deus absconditus* who illuminates the darkness by the traces of his absence.

So much for these general remarks. One does not have to be a Heideggerian in order to see (or should I say "hear") that he makes an important point. We have little or no evidence that the fullness of vision or pure illumination is available to human beings. If it is, there seems to be no end to a discursive account of what we have seen. This is true of Plato as well as of Husserlian phenomenology. But it is also true of Heidegger; the ontological analysis contained in *Being and Time* is valid only for the present epoch of the history of Being. And even if the ecstatic structure of temporality should be perpetual, like Nietzsche's eternal return, what returns is not the determinate content of each moment, as Nietzsche's Zarathustra claims, but a temporal space for the actualization of new possibilities, or endless finite discourses.[21]

---

21 This is clear in Heidegger's peculiar definition of the *Augenblick* or authentic present, not as a *jetzt* or a *nun* or a place in which something occurs: "but as authentic *Gegen-wart*, it first allows that to occur which can be 'in a time' as *Zuhandenes* or *Vorhandenes*." That is to say, it allows *Dasein* to encounter authentic possibilities See 338/388).

What is at stake here is not whether Plato was a crypto-Nietzschean but whether his actual teaching takes account of the correlative roles of presence and absence. I think we can find evidence that it does. In order to do so, we must turn from the Ideas to the soul, and therefore, to the doctrine of eros. The function of eros does not play an important role in Heidegger's discussions of Plato, although there is a kind of surrogate for eros in Heidegger's own concept of *Sorge* (care). It would take me too far afield to discuss the differences between eros and *Sorge* in any detail, but it is obvious that they represent two quite different attunements of the human soul. Eros, I think it is fair to say, has a connection with happiness and playfulness that is totally missing in *Sorge*. Even Fichte's *Streben* (striving) and certainly Nietzsche's *Wille zur Macht* (will to power) seem to be closer to eros than is *Sorge*.

Eros carries the human soul up toward the Ideas. In the *Symposium* Diotima explicitly instructs Socrates that eros, namely, the human soul, is continuously changing from life to death,[22] and that love, the fundamental characteristic of the soul, is the desire for what one does not possess. In the highest and the only truly satisfying instance, the objects of desire are the Ideas, represented here by the Idea of beauty. But this leads directly to a serious difficulty for Heidegger's major criticism of Platonism. If the soul continues to shift back and forth from life to death even when it has seen the Idea of beauty, that vision will be punctuated by intervals of absence. On the other hand, if the vision of the Idea of beauty satisfies the soul's erotic appetite, then eros can no longer exist, which surely means that the soul will perish. On this alternative, philosophy is not simply the preparation for dying, as Socrates says in the *Phaedo*; it is death itself. Full presence is replaced by full absence, at least in this world.

The truth is that Diotima's formulation of this point is surprisingly close to Heidegger. To be present to the light is also to have

---

22 *Symp.* 203e1–3 (eros is between life and death; it changes its form in the same day from one to the other); cf. 207d6–e5 (human beings are continuously dying and being reborn in body and soul).

overcome the concealment of absence. Human being, as represented by eros, is marked by an "ontological" restlessness that is obviously connected very closely to our temporality. In the
Symposium, the restlessness of eros is camouflaged as the production of true instances of virtue. Socrates expresses the same point
in the *Republic* by introducing the notion of the soul as divided
within itself by a struggle for dominance between the eros of intellect and the *eros turannos* of the desires, a struggle that can be
resolved only by the intervention of spiritedness on behalf of intellect.

In Socratic language, the human soul is ill and can be healed
only by philosophy, which in turn rests upon dialectic or the
knowledge of Ideas. The possibility of dialectic is asserted in one
of the most enigmatic passages in the Platonic corpus.[23] One is
forced to wonder whether the claim to possess the science of
dialectic is not another of the notorious noble lies of the philosopher-kings in the just city. But even if the claim can be fulfilled, the
order in the soul, and therefore in the city, is not resolved but kept
under control by rhetorical and physical compulsion. The vision
of the Ideas does not heal; it subdues. This is to say that darkness
cannot be expunged from the soul.

To come back to the issue of temporality, at the highest stage
in her description of erotic ascent, Diotima refers twice to philosophy, or rather once to philosophy and once to dialectic. In the
first reference, we behold the sea of the beautiful and give birth
"in ungrudging philosophy to many beautiful speeches and
thoughts" (*dianoêmata*).[24] In the second reference, Diotima
speaks of the acquisition of "a certain single philosophical science," presumably dialectic, that provides us with the ultimate
vision of the unchanging and homogeneous Idea of beauty.[25]

In both cases, the soul engages in acts of generation. The products of the penultimate stage are "phantom images" (*eidôla*), like

23 R. VI. 510b4–9. Cf. 505a5ff: we have no adequate knowledge of the Good.
    This deprives our knowledge of Ideas of utility, beauty, and goodness.
24 *Symp.* 210d3–6.
25 Ibid. 210d7.

those generated in the lower stages. Only in the ultimate stage are our productions true. Nevertheless, our function as human beings is not simply to contemplate the Idea of beauty, but to generate in its light.[26] Since these generations can neither add to nor fully duplicate the Idea of beauty, they must be partial representations of it. In other words, even if we could see the Idea of beauty in its full presence, we would be unable to represent it in any human speech or deed. There is nothing to count or measure here. Just because geometrical forms and properties are beautiful, this does not mean that the Idea of beauty is a geometrical form. As described by Diotima, the Idea of beauty has no individuating characteristics. The beautiful productions of human beings are individuated by temporality.

This point is made still more explicit in the *Phaedrus* where Socrates says that even the divine souls that easily reach the roof of the cosmos see the hyperuranian beings *dia chronou*, "through the medium of time," which must therefore extend beyond the roof of the rotating cosmos, and thus serves as an impediment to the full presence of the Ideas.[27] This is a rather Heideggerean passage, but one which he does not exploit, so far as I recall, perhaps because it would contradict his interpretation of Plato. As to the best human souls, they are able to stick their heads up intermittently through the roof of the cosmos, and in addition their vision is disturbed by the jostling of their own passions as well as by the attempt of the other souls to rise to the top.[28]

Let me now summarize my lecture to this point. I have introduced the dialectic of light and darkness by means of a general assessment of Heidegger's critical interpretation of Platonism. The upshot of this assessment is that Plato indicates the Heideggerean problematic in mythical or poetical terms in the *Symposium, Phaedrus, and Republic*, to mention only these dialogues. In the first two, Plato portrays the reciprocity of light and darkness as a

---

26 Ibid. 212a2–7. I follow Benardete's translation of eidôla.
27 *Phdr.* 247c1–2, d3.
28 Ibid. 248a1–b5.

function of the temporality of eros. In the *Republic*, the point is made with respect to the dialectic of the soul, and the problem is suggested by the fact that eros is both used to characterize the pursuit of knowledge by the philosophical nature and denigrated as the most tyrannical of the desires.

We are assured by Socrates that whenever the soul fixes its eyes upon what is lit up by truth and genuine being, "it engages in pure thought and knows it, and appears to possess pure intellect" (*enoêsen te kai egnô auto kai noun echein phainetai*).[29] This is a rather ambiguous statement, more hopeful than unqualifiedly declarative. But even if we take it as a genuine Platonic endorsement of the full presence of the Ideas to the master of dialectic, and thereby ignore the degree in which the entire conversation is portrayed as difficult to distinguish from wishing,[30] we must still reconcile this passage with the radical discontinuity between erotic existence and the faculty of *noêsis*.

I turn now to what is for Heidegger himself the most important Platonic statement on light and darkness: the image of the cave in Book Seven of the *Republic*. Heidegger sees in this text "an unspoken . . . turning-point in the definition of the essence of the truth" (*PLW*, 201/155), that is, from truth as *Unverborgenheit* (the grasping of truth from the darkness) to truth as correctness (*PLW*, 228/176ff), with a subsequent suppression of absence or concealment in favor of full presence. By "unspoken" Heidegger means that Plato is himself unaware of this change. I shall in effect argue that no such turn, spoken or unspoken, takes place.

Let us begin by reminding ourselves of the architecture of the cave. Socrates says that we are to "construct an image of [*apeikason*] our nature with respect to its formation [*paideia*] and lack of formation" (514a1–2). The verb *apeikason* is an echo of the immediately preceding reference at the end of Book VI to *eikasia*,

---

29 VI. 508d6.
30 Consider VII. 540d1–5. [Ed.: The reference is to the following statement by Socrates: "What then?," I said. "Do you not agree that the things we have said about the city and the regime are not in every way prayers; that they are hard but in a way possible.]

the lowest segment on the so-called divided line or rank ordering of human faculties (511e2). According to Heidegger, *paideia* means in this text what will shortly be referred to as the *periagôge holês tês psuchês*, that is, the turning round of human nature from the shadows projected onto the wall of the cave to the vision of Platonic Ideas (*PLW*, 215/166).

Heidegger correctly raises the question whether it is appropriate to entrust the account of human transformation to an image, but he seems to imply that the oddness of this choice is to be explained by an unconscious inner transformation within Plato's thought concerning the nature of truth (*PLW,* 216/167). It remains to be seen whether there is anything to this claim. But I believe that there is another, more obvious point to be made. The representation of the faculties of the soul by a divided line is itself an icon, and one which assigns the lowest rank to the production of images. The reliance placed by Socrates upon images makes it clear that there is something incomplete and misleading about his account, not just of images, but more generally, of poetry and production. As I argued in my second lecture, this defect is not something unnoticed by Plato but instead arises from the general political program of the *Republic*.

From a Heideggerean perspective, one might wish to contend that the reliance upon poetry and images shows Plato's unconscious shifting from pre-Socratic doctrines of uncoveredness or disclosure to a metaphysics of production. In my view, it shows rather that Plato must rehabilitate poetry in its proper function: that of disclosing or uncovering the nature of the human soul. It is not the soul that is produced, but rather the instruments by which we explain, to ourselves and others, what we have discovered. The image of the divided line, like that of the cave, is certainly a human production, but the original corresponding to the produced image is no more produced itself than is a body produced by viewing its reflection in a mirror or on the surface of a pond.

Differently stated, images are not all imitations in the crude sense that a reflection is an imitation of one's face. In this sense, there are no images of the human soul. No one would suggest that the soul is, or looks like, a cave full of prisoners or a winged charioteer. Yet it is not difficult to see the aspect of human nature that the image illuminates. I discussed this question last time and will return to it in my final lecture.

I turn next to the relation between the image of the cave and its original. At 517a8–518d7, in a passage paraphrased by Heidegger, Socrates identifies the main elements in the image as follows. The prison home or cave corresponds to the domain that is revealed through sight and the firelight within the cave represents the power of the sun. The journey of the released prisoner upward, out of the cave and into the sunlight, represents the journey of the soul up to "the intelligible place" (*ton noêton topon*).

Heidegger infers from this that the cave represents "everyday" (*alltäglich*) life, and that the vault of the cave corresponds to the vault of the heavens. The mode of Being of the things with which they carry out their everyday tasks is characterized by Heidegger as *das Seiende*. (*PLW*, 211–212/164). This reminds us of the property of "being at hand" that plays a central role in the analysis of everydayness in *Being and Time*. The German expression designates the mode of Being of what in Greek would be called *onta*. Accordingly, the entities external to the cave represent the Platonic Ideas, *das eigentlich Seiende des Seienden* or that through which the things of everyday life present themselves in their look (*Aussehen*) as that which is truly or genuinely.

I have two comments about the Heideggerian reading of the image to this point. The first is that, by identifying the cave with everyday life, Heidegger oversimplifies the extremely complex structure of the image. For example, he is silent about the degree to which the cave is intended to represent the city. Otherwise put, politics is reduced by implication to the domain of the everyday and so to the inauthentic. It should be said that there is a problem with taking the cave as simply equivalent to the city, but this does not permit us to ignore the connection altogether. I will clarify this point in my next lecture.

There is a second and related problem for which Heidegger's analysis does not prepare us. As he puts it, the shadows cast upon the rear wall of the cave correspond to *das Seiende*, i.e., the things or *onta* of everyday life, whereas the things outside the cave represent the Platonic Ideas and the sun that illuminates them represents the Idea of the Good (*PLW*, 211–213/165). It follows that there are four main elements in the image, which we can say is also a proportion. As the Idea of the Good is to the Ideas, so is the sun to the objects on the surface of the earth.

The problem is that the proportion external to the cave does not correspond to its interior. The shadows on the wall of the cave do not correspond to sunlit external objects; this role is played by the artifacts carried around behind the backs of, and invisible to, the prisoners chained to their seats. Furthermore, the shadows are cast by an artificial fire and are thus artificial or let us say "artifactual" in a way that sunlit objects are not. If we stand in the sunlight on the surface of the earth and see a tree, we also see its shadow, which is so to speak "attached" to the tree as perceived. Inside the cave, we see the shadow of an artifactual tree, but as completely independent of the manufactured tree, which is not visible to the prisoners. And the same is true of the artificial fire, which is not seen at all until the prisoner is released from his chains. In viewing the objects of the surface world, however, we also see the sun.

Heidegger's interpretation is in a way obvious, and it certainly corresponds to Socrates' own account of the function of the image. The problem is that the interpretation does not coincide with the details of the image. As soon as we begin to consider these details, the coherence of the interpretation dissolves. The life of the prisoners inside the cave is supposed to represent "everyday" life on the surface of the earth, whereas the surface life within the image stands for the domain of the Platonic Ideas. This raises two related questions. First: does the image of cave life correspond to the broad structure of actual surface life? Second: does the image of surface life correspond generally to the domain of the Ideas? The answer to the second question is certainly negative. The released prisoner is presented as ascending within the sunlight from shadows to images to things as they are (515e6–516b7). In other words, the part of the image that supposedly corresponds to the sphere of the Ideas is in fact a description of the transition from everyday surface life to the highest sphere.

As to the first question, I have already commented on the difference between shadows inside and those outside the cave. The shadows of the sunlight are naturally produced and connected to their bodies; the shadows within the cave are artificially produced and detached from their bodies, which are invisible to the prisoners. If the cave-life represents our "everyday" or pre-philosophical condition, then the process of cognition at this stage depends upon the production of shadows of artifacts manipulated by puppeteers. In other words, we prisoners are ourselves the puppeteers who produce the domain of shadows cast by puppets or figurines that are in turn images of things as they are. In short, pre-philosophical cognition is indeed productive. But the whole point of the doctrine of Ideas is to refute the metaphysics of production, and it does this by distinguishing between Being and the images of the various stages in the cognitive process, from which we escape only through the vision of the Ideas.

This interpretation is not flawless, nor is it intended as a complete identification of the significance of the puppet-masters. But it seems to account for the various elements in the description of cave life in a manner that is both coherent and compatible with, if not indeed required by, the doctrine of Ideas as presented in the middle books of the *Republic*. As I understand it, the portrait of cave life does not represent the "everyday" sphere as something we transcend in our ascent to the Ideas. It is rather an image of the structure of the psychology of cognition. The human being is a creature of shadows, which affect even our vision of the Ideas. But the Ideas are not shadows; on the contrary, they provide us with the possibility of understanding ourselves, and to that extent freeing ourselves from the limitation of shadow-vision.

Furthermore, as we shall see next time, the released prisoner must be forced to avert his eyes from the shadows toward the puppets, and then to ascend to the surface world of sunlight. This is to say that, as Heidegger claims on behalf of the original or pre-

Platonist view, the acquisition of truth is a wresting of disclosed-ness (*Entringung jeweils in der Weise der Entbergen*): "truth signifies originally that which is wrested from hiddenness" (*das einer Verborgenheit Abgerungene*")(*PLW*, 221/171). But this is one of the most important themes of the image of the cave. And it is supported by the previously cited evidence from the *Symposium* and *Phaedrus*, as well as from the *Republic* itself.

I will continue my analysis next time. Meanwhile I hope to have persuaded you that speleology is more difficult than ontology.

Lecture Four:
In and Out of the Cave

In *Platons Lehre von der Wahrheit*, Heidegger distinguishes four different stages in the cave allegory, which he says correspond to four different senses of *Unverborgenheit* or *das offen Anwesende*. These stages are associated with (1) the vision of the shadows; (2) the initial access to the artificially illuminated objects (the statuettes) corresponding to the shadows of stage one; (3) the vision of the Ideas; and (4) the return of the released prisoner into the cave to attempt to free the remaining prisoners.

This division is not without its difficulties. Heidegger himself admits that there is no reference to "truth" and so to *Unverborgenheit* in his stage four (*PLW*, 221/171), nor was I able to find this term in stage three. In fact, just which part of the text corresponds to stage three is blurred by an almost complete absence of page references to the Greek (*PLW*, 219–220/169–170).[1] Furthermore, what Heidegger calls the third stage is a combination of two stages, namely, the released prisoner's vision of sun-illuminated objects and his ascent to the sun itself. As to stage four, that is not a new and higher type of *Unverborgenheit* but a descent to a lower and previously accomplished stage.

---

1   Heidegger cites only *R.* 516a3, where Socrates refers to "what is now said to be true," namely, the objects on the surface or in the sunlight in contrast to the objects within the cave. This does not refer to Platonic Ideas.

Heidegger apparently takes stage two (initial perception of the cave artifacts) to represent the vision of objects on the earth's surface. But there is a lack of symmetry between the elements of the cave image and their intended originals. Stages (1) and (2) inside the cave do not correspond to their ostensible originals (1) and (2) outside the cave. The statuettes carried by the so-called puppet-masters inside the cave include those of "all kinds of *skeuê*" as well as of human beings and other animals. *Skeuos* has a wide range of meanings, but its primary sense is that of household implements. "Some of the carriers of puppets utter sounds, whereas others are silent" (VII. 514b8–515a3). There are no statues of non-sentient natural things or processes. Once again, the mechanics of the cave image rules out the possibility of shadows of the heavens, the elements, and so on. The noises associated with the animals are "sounds," i.e., the difference between animals with *logos* and those without is not captured in the initial setting of the image. This suggests that the implements represented are those of pre-political life.

Perhaps the most puzzling feature of the cave image is the question how the prisoners could make any sense at all of the shadows, since their chains make it impossible for them to see anything but themselves and the shadows on the back wall of the cave. Needless to say, there are no puppets of the heavenly bodies or natural elements. The more closely we examine the details of the cave image, the clearer it becomes that there is no direct relation of image and original between the interior of the cave and everyday life, as Heidegger seems to believe.[2] It is true that Socrates refers to the prisoners in the cave as human beings like us (514a2, b8, 515a5). But he is representing fundamental elements of cognition, and in particular the perceptual process at a pre-discursive or pre-"logical" stage, not the everyday life of fully developed human beings.

I shall refer to the cave as the sub-natural dimension of human perception. By "sub-natural" I mean something like what

2   *PLW*, 211–212/164–165.

Heidegger describes as the darkness from which the truth must be grasped and brought into the light. But the cave is of course not completely dark; the sounds of the puppeteers stand to human *logos* as does the firelight in the cave to the sun in the outer world. This brings me to two closely related questions. Who are the puppet-masters, and who has produced their puppets? My answer, to be developed directly, is as follows: The puppet-masters are not separate from their prisoners but combine with them in an image of the original process of perception. It is this process that produces the puppets, but not the natural beings of which they are representations.

Accordingly, I reject the interpretation of the puppet-masters as the opinion-makers of the city who impress their views onto the deluded citizenry. This interpretation is unacceptable; there is no reference here to opinions and none to political activity, but only to sense perception. It follows immediately from the text that the shadows are a defining feature of perceptible entities whose existence can be explained by the combined activity of the puppet-masters and their slaves. Let me underline this remark: *Each of us is both a puppeteer and a prisoner.* We must ourselves be "torn" from our chains in order to negotiate the ascent into the sunlight, but for reasons which, as we shall see, Socrates never makes entirely clear, the philosopher must return into the cave and converse with his former fellow prisoners in the attempt to free them from their own shadows. But this is a shadow that falls over philosophy, which cannot remain entirely within the sunlight. Contrary to Heidegger's usual assertions, the Platonism of Socrates submits to the intrinsic interplay between light and darkness that is cognitively manifested in the dialogue between perception and noetic intuition.

This is another way of saying that there is no fourth stage of ultimate or complete *Unverborgenheit* in the allegory of the cave. It is no accident that the "political" aspect of the allegory begins precisely with the descent of the philosopher back into the cave. One can also say that the way up is not the same as the way down. I am of course not entirely serious here when I suggest that

Heidegger is too receptive to the teaching of Heraclitus. What is entirely certain, nevertheless, is that Heidegger stakes everything on the claim that there is a progressive movement within the allegory of the cave toward an ever more correct type of vision, and that this movement culminates in the replacement of the original Greek doctrine of truth as uncoveredness or unconcealment by truth as correctness (*PLW*, 227–228/175–176). Accordingly, truth, which is now understood as the Platonic Idea, loses its original connection with concealment, and so with the struggle by which the visible is wrested or torn from the dark. I am in the process of denying this general assertion.

It would have been better for Heidegger to say that the return of the freed man or philosopher into the cave represents the impossibility of detaching full vision or correctness from the domain of shadows. This has something essential to do with the relation between philosophy and politics. Socrates does not say that the philosopher, as we may fairly call him, is compelled to return into the cave. Instead, he describes what would happen *if* there were such a return (*ei palin*: 516e3). In fact, the same formulation is used with respect to each stage of the prisoner's release and ascent. If compulsion is applied, then the upward journey will be carried out. But this is not a matter of personal decision; the compulsion is external. And in fact, it is rarely applied. In the case of descent, the situation is more complicated. In order to understand it, we must move beyond the technical issue of visual or noetic perception to the relations between philosophy and politics. This reflection is not necessary with respect to the ascent. Those who, like Heidegger, entirely ignore the political dimension of the cave image are as mistaken as those who understand the cave to be identical with the city. In sum, part one of the cave image represents the sub-natural foundation of perceptual awareness, and part two, from which the puppet-masters are entirely absent, introduces the sub-natural transition to social and political intercourse.

According to Socrates, philosophers who live in actual cities have no obligation to participate in government, and would do so at peril to their lives. Their ascent to the Ideas is not a consequence of the laws of the city, but of their own nature, or, as Socrates describes his own case, thanks to the intervention of the *daimonion*. On the other hand, those philosophers who have been raised and educated in the just city are obligated to repay the government for the opportunity to live a philosophical life. They are therefore compelled to rule, that is, to return to the cave, which remains the psychological or cognitive condition of the non-philosophers. The fourth stage of the cave image indicates what fate would await the returning philosophers were not the just city already under the authority of philosopher-kings. This authority, of course, is represented elsewhere in the *Republic* as the persuasion of spiritedness by intellect to regulate and suppress the passions of the soul. Since the just city does not exist, it follows that should philosophers choose to participate in politics, as did Plato himself on two occasions, they do so on their own volition. And they have nothing to expect but the fate that nearly cost Plato his life.

Before I leave this point, I want to mention that, if Socrates is correct in his contention that philosophers will decline to participate in the rule of actual cities, then the just city seems to be impossible. The beautiful city (*kallipolis*) must be founded by a philosopher, but this requires the overthrow of an existing city, as is obvious from the need to expel everyone over the age of ten and to control every aspect of the nurture and education of the remaining children. More generally expressed, the cave image either ignores politics and concentrates upon the *periagôgê* of the individual soul, or, as in the descent scene, it emphasizes the antagonism between philosophy and politics.

Let me restate the main point concerning the peculiarity of the architecture of the cave image. In actual life, according to Socrates, there are two kinds of objects, those of the domain of genesis and the Platonic Ideas. To these there correspond two kinds of "objective" perception: sense perception and noetic intuition. The objects of sense perception are like shadows of the objects of *noêsis*. Finally, within the domain of genesis, the sun

stands to objects of sense perception as does the Idea of the Good
to the Ideas in the domain of eternity. The shadows of sunlight are
normally perceived as connected to the objects of sense perception. But the shadows within the cave are for the prisoners percep-
tually entirely distinct from their artifactual originals, which are
not seen at all. Otherwise put, the cave shadows are of puppets
which are themselves copies of artifacts and sentient beings of the
normal or generated sort. The viewing of shadows in the cave is
thus the perception of copies of copies. It is nothing like the perception of objects, but more like mistaking one's reflection in a
pool for an actual face. It is therefore misleading to identify the
first stage within the cave image with some actual perceptual or
cognitive state. The viewing of shadows is more like a basis step
in a procedure that retains the shadows at all higher levels. This is
the symbolic significance of the fact that in the actual world, shadows are re-attached, i.e., perceived together with, actual bodies.
And the shadows remain even in the intuition of Ideas, as we have
already had occasion to notice.

When Socrates says that the cave image represents "our
nature" with respect to *paideia* and *apaideusia* (514a1–2), and
again that the cave dwellers are "like us" (515a5), he certainly
does not mean that each stage in the image is an imitation of a historical stage in human life. I have already discussed in a previous
lecture the weakness of the paradigm of mimesis with respect to
the arts, and the same point holds good for images. To say that the
soul is a winged charioteer driving two horses, one noble and the
other base, is of course not to assert that the image is a copy of the
soul. The image is meant to show what cannot be captured by a
perfect duplication, rather than to supply that duplicate. One
could say that the function of the image is to render visible what
is itself concealed or absent. This bears some similarity to the
Heideggerian notion of truth as having been wrested from concealment.

It should be emphasized that, as Heidegger correctly notes,
paideia does not mean here "education" in a doctrine but refers
instead to the formation through which the soul is "turned

entirely around" (*periagôgê holês tês psuchês*) from the domain of shadows to the sphere of the Ideas (*PLW*, 215–216/166–167). In other words, the cave image is neither ontological nor epistemological, but it represents the psychological preconditions for a *logos* of the Ideas. This precondition is not pure openness or *Lichtung* but something like the darkness of a cave that is partially illuminated by firelight. To say that light depends upon openness is to imply that openness is itself preceded by the closure of darkness. Human existence begins in the partly illuminated space between these two extremes. And this is as true for Plato as it is for Heidegger. Each act of cognition is a re-enactment of the interplay of light and darkness, of the attempt by light to escape from darkness, and of its being forced to return to the cave.

For all the reasons that have been mentioned to this point, we should not be surprised to find that the life of the cave dwellers is not at all an imitation of "everyday life." The proportion between the interior and the exterior worlds is symbolic, not arithmetical. For example, as we have just noticed, whereas the sun stands for natural genesis, its ostensible image, the firelight within the cave, illuminates artifacts, namely, the figurines carried by the puppeteers, figurines of which only the shadows are visible to the bound cave-dwellers. This points to the fact that there is no genesis or growth in the cave, and no eros, nor is there any reference to decay and death. The shadows inside the cave are not the same as images in the domain of the sunlight, because firelight is not a fully adequate image of sunlight. Nature within the cave is not the *phusis* of the domain of sunlight. This is why I have referred to it as "sub-natural" or representative of the primordial level of the human soul. By the very fact of the correlation between the outer world and the cave, we cannot detach ourselves from this foundation but must take it with us when we enter the domain of the sun. To do so, however, is not to reduce one to the other, but to preserve the depth of our being as creatures of light and darkness.

As a second example, let us reconsider the identity of the puppeteers, who are referred to as "human beings" (*anthrôpous*) at 514b8, and the initially tempting hypothesis that they stand for a separate class of persons in everyday life who deceive us into believing that the shadows of their figurines are real objects. There are of course masters of opinion who can be said to delude the multitude; one has only to think of the philosopher-kings in Socrates' just city. But this identification is not plausible for a reason that I have already given. The mistake of the prisoners is perceptual, not ideological. The shadows are of objects, and in the sense of projections of perception, they are not shadows of correct opinions about politics and virtue. More generally, to take literally the human identity of the puppeteers is to treat the cave as the image of the city. I have already suggested that this cannot account for the entire allegory, and this is especially true in the first half of the image.

To begin with, there is no political life in the original disposition of the cave; this is ruled out by the conditions of bondage, which make it impossible for human intercourse of any kind, even of the kind appropriate to slaves. In particular, there is little if any reference to speech among the prisoners prior to the return of the former prisoner and no such reference at all with respect to the puppeteers. In fact, the only human activity within the cave to this point in the allegory is the upward ascent of the released prisoner from firelight to sunlight. This is not political but rather the rejection of politics. Nor, as we shall see shortly, does the descent of the released prisoner back into the cave establish it as an icon of the city. Otherwise put, justice is not the theme of the image of the cave. As Socrates says, those who have seen the Idea of the Good are unwilling to mind the business of human beings but must apparently be compelled to do so (517c7–9). This is a clear anticipation of what will later be said of the philosopher-kings, with the major exception that the latter are compelled by justice to return to the city, whereas no reason is given for the return of the released cave dweller.

If the image of the cave has a political message, it is surely negative rather than positive; politics and philosophy are incompatible. Someone might object that we can remove this incompatibility by making philosophers kings. But this would be to forget the amount of duplicity, not to mention compulsion, that the latter are forced to employ in the attempt to preserve justice. The rule of philosophers looks suspiciously like the exchange of one set of puppet-masters for another. However this may be, it is largely irrelevant to our immediate task. We need only to see that the cave cannot be equated with the city, and so that the puppet- masters are not statesmen, whether virtuous or vicious. On the other hand, as we shall see shortly, the theme of political life arises in the second half of the myth.

I have suggested that the puppet-masters do not represent a real class of persons in the outer world, but that their presence in the myth, together with their figurines, is required in order to construct a dramatic portrait of the perceptual error that characterizes life in the cave. Puppeteers and prisoners combine to produce shadow-vision. This vision is rooted in the depths of human nature. It is not a result of the indoctrination of one part of the city by another. There are, then, not two types of human being in the cave, but one type containing two natures: master and slave. The incompleteness of each part is represented by their fetishes, as one might call them: puppets and shadows of puppets.

If I may take another step into the twilight of speculation, the puppet-masters and prisoners represent something like what Hegel refers to in the *Phenomenology of Spirit* as the dialectic of master and slave, understanding these as two dimensions of the individual soul. For Hegel, the resolution of this dialectic lies in the inversion of roles: the slave becomes master and the master is enslaved. For Socrates, the master undergoes his own kind of slavery by being forced to rule through compulsion and noble lies. This is as true in the domain of perception as it is in politics. That it holds for the individual human being is in the case of Plato evident in the tripartition of the soul in the *Republic*, in which reason rules desire through the mediation of spiritedness.

In fact, according to the *Republic* as a whole, correct perception depends upon politics, namely, upon the establishment of the rule of philosophers and their elaborate education. Conversely, these depend upon the compulsion exerted upon potential philosophers to accept political rule, or in other words, upon the antecedent existence of the just city. This circularity leaves it quite dubious that the just city can ever be established, but that is a topic for a different lecture. To stay with our main point, Socrates elsewhere refers to the just relation within the soul between the ruling part and the natural slaves.[3] The present reference to the same metaphor has to do with the process by which perception constructs its objects. The element of the master produces the shadows of perception and the prisoner or slave takes these shadows for reality. In other words, just as the sun is the original of which the firelight is the image, so the objects illuminated by the sun are shadows in comparison to the Ideas. But just as the released prisoner is apparently compelled to return to the cave, so the philosophers are compelled to return to the domain of the sun, and not just to return, but, as human beings, to spend most of their lives in its light. To know that we are surrounded by shadows is not the same thing as to be free of them. In the transition to sunlight, we carry the cave with us.

Let us now look more carefully at the release of the prisoner from his chains. This liberation is presented as effected by nature and is instantaneous (*eksaiphnês*). That is to say, nature forces the released prisoner to stand up as soon as the chains are broken, and to look around the cave (515c4–7). At the same instant, the puppet-masters disappear from the scene. The released prisoner is now potentially his own master. But this does not mean that the shadows disappear as well. Mastery or liberty refers to the capacity to engage in war with the shadows. As I pointed out previously, to know that we are deluded by shadows is not the same as to be entirely free of them.

The preconditions for the perceptual illusion are no longer in full effect. But the former prisoner is not prepared to leave the cave with the same suddenness that marked his release. He is too disoriented to take in the actual identity of the artifacts and their shadows. Therefore, force must be applied (515c6, e1, e6) at each

3   Cf. *R*, IV, 444b4–5.

stage of this transitional period that culminates in the ascent to the entrance of the cave. What is the source of this force?

I note that there is no "method" or set of discursive arguments by which we shift from shadows to objects. But neither can it be accomplished through the agency of our former masters or fellow prisoners. It seems to be an inexplicable manifestation of sub-natural power. In the outer world, Socrates would call it eros, which makes its first appearance in the cave image through an anonymous or concealed surrogate. Among the missing features are sexual desire and love of the beautiful. This reinforces my choice of the term "sub-natural" to describe the function of nature within the cave.

Having been liberated from his chains, the former prisoner begins to walk about the cave and is subjected to the pain of unused muscles as well as to the dazzling effect of the firelight upon eyes that were habituated to shadows (515c3–d1). Socrates imagines a dialogue between the released prisoner and an unidentified interlocutor who is familiar with the actual source of the shadows on the cave wall. If the interlocutor were to explain to our hero the difference between shadows and artifacts, it would be to no avail. The reason, of course, is because we must first see before we can distinguish between appearance and reality. Once again: openness is the condition of discourse. There is no difference between Plato and the pre-Socratics on the topic of *Unverborgenheit*.

At this point, the attempt at (hypothetical) persuasion ceases and force enters into the picture. Initially, the interlocutor compels the released cave dweller to look at "the light" (i.e., the firelight). But this causes pain and the former prisoner struggles to turn back to the shadows with which he is familiar (515d1–e5). If someone were then to drag him out of the cave and into the domain of the sun, vision would not be immediate. In other words, release from one's chains is only the first step in philosophical *paideia*. We still require the application of external force. I take this to refer to the force of eros rather than to any actual person, say, a teacher. The former prisoner is still too disoriented to respond to persuasion.

The second step in philosophical *paideia* is, as it were, physiological or even existential rather than doctrinal.

Another striking point in this passage is that the interlocutor does not mention human beings but limits himself to showing our hero the artifacts that were previously transported by the puppet-masters. Human beings are mentioned only as objects of perception, distinguished from their shadows and phantoms (*eidôla*: distorted images) in the course of one's becoming accustomed to the sunlight (516a5–8). Again, the progress out of the cave is not political but concerns the private development of the potential philosopher. Discourse is subordinated to perception, but as we saw a moment ago, perception is itself dependent upon the openness of the illuminated horizon. In other words, Plato is presenting a rather Heideggerian account of the dependence of perceptual and discursive truth upon vision. The corollary to this is the interplay of shadows and light at each stage of psychological development.

After the ex-prisoner becomes accustomed to the sunlight, his vision gradually sharpens, and he moves from shadows and reflections to the objects, natural and artificial, of the visible domain, next, to heavenly bodies, and finally, to the sun and sunlight (516a5–b2). In this way he gradually acquires a correct picture of the physical cosmos, and with it, happiness that arises from comparing his present lot with that of the prisoners below. I note the appearance of the term *sullogizoito* at 516b9: calculation or computation begins in connection with the motions of the heavenly bodies, that is, when perception has been clarified. At this point, the character of the myth changes. The happiness of the free man is mitigated by pity for those who are still imprisoned within the cave (516c6). This is the first sign of an interest in his fellow human beings. Let me call it the pre-political stage of the cave image; pity is not the same as, but may lead to, a desire for justice.

In keeping with the aforementioned change, Socrates now asks us to suppose that the cave dwellers have honors, praises, and prizes for those who see most sharply what passes by (*ta parionta*: 516c9). One would assume that these are the shadows cast by the puppets that are carried around (*tôn pariontôn*: 515d4; *tôn parapherontôn*: 515a3, b2) by the puppet-master, rather than the puppets themselves, since the prisoners have not yet been released. On the other hand, they are now aware of their neighbors and able to converse with them, which was not possible in the initial description of cave life. Thus, at 515b4, Socrates asks what would happen "if it were possible for [the chained prisoners] to converse with one another," thereby indicating that they cannot. At 516c8ff, Socrates asks what would happen if there were competitions and prizes within the cave for correct perceptual identification. The context leaves it unclear whether this refers to the first or the second stage of the image, but the second alternative is suggested by the nature of the limited powers of the fully bound prisoners. The distribution of honors, praises, and prizes for keenness of perception is an extension of the proto-political nature of this segment of the allegory, but we should remember that the concern for justice is not said to be present. On the contrary, the former prisoner would not be desirous or envious of the lot of the most perspicuous of the cave dwellers, and in particular, he would not desire to rule them (*endunasteuontas*: 516d4). Socrates emphasizes the point by adding, with the assistance of a citation from Homer, that the free man would undergo anything rather than to live in that way, and Glaucon concurs (516d4–e2). The life of a penniless serf on the soil of the earth is preferable to that of a king within the cave.

Why then does the free man descend back into the cave, with the inevitable result that his perception of the shadows is blurred by the absence of light? The text suggests that he has been motivated by pity to attempt to release his former companions, who strongly resist and would even attempt to kill him if they could (516e3–517a6). This passage is an unmistakable allusion to the fate of Socrates in Athens, and it confirms the antagonism between politics and philosophy. The antagonism is not strong enough to prevent the philosopher from attempting to educate his fellow citizens, and thus to lead them at least partially out of the cave.

I continue to understand this passage as proto-political, but not political in the full sense, because teaching is combined (at least by Socrates) with a refusal to hold political office. Furthermore, even and especially within the just city, there is a fundamental difference between the education of the potential philosophers and that of the non-philosophers. In sum, we are allowed to attribute the descent into the cave to philanthropy, and to assume that the improvement of one's fellow humans is also beneficial for oneself. But there is another consideration. It is the nature of human existence that the philosopher cannot devote his entire life to the contemplation of the Ideas. Even assuming that these are intermittently available to *noêsis*, we must all return to the cave, and the struggle with the domain of shadows occurs within each of us, including the lover of wisdom. This is the human expression of the technical point that a full *parousia* in Heidegger's sense is impossible.

In sum, the return into the cave is sudden (*eksaiphnês*: 516e5), and therefore it blinds us, just as we were blinded by the sudden (*eksaiphnês*: 515c6) release from our chains and the initial view of the firelight. Philosophy does not provide us with immunity from the disorientation of cave vision. This shifting back and forth is presumably a part of the *paideia* with which the entire allegory was said to be concerned. Once more, there is no reference to a doctrine or a method for negotiating the shift. Nor could this be attributed to philosophical eros, which leads us up out of the cave, not down into it. Perhaps we can suggest that pity is the Platonic preparation for what Heidegger calls *Sorge*. The difference between the two seems to be that pity is directed toward others by its very nature, whereas *Sorge* is fundamentally concerned with one's ownmost existence.

One thing is clear. The only occurrence of conversation inside the cave, prior to the descent, is hypothetical. Socrates asks what the newly released prisoner would say *if* someone were to ask him what each thing is (*hoti estin*). He would be at a loss to reply because his eyes were dazzled by the firelight (515c9–d7). The emphasis throughout is upon the identification of perceptual objects, and this is no doubt what led Heidegger to interpret the underlying shift from the view of truth as *Unverborgenheit* to the correct description of reified aspects of perception. On my reading, the image preserves its inherent unity, despite all elaborations and in particular, despite the shift from the apolitical to the political.

I want to add the following remark about Heidegger's identification of the primordial Greek view of truth as unconcealedness, from which Plato ostensibly deviates. I am not concerned with the historical accuracy of this identification but with its philosophical soundness. Heidegger is right to say that we cannot formulate propositional statements about something unless it lies open before us as that to which we refer. But Plato does not overlook this rather obvious point. It is dramatically illustrated by the silence within the cave in the initial condition of bondage, and by the *aporia* (515d6) faced by the released prisoner when he is asked to say "what is it?" with respect to each of the artifacts of the puppet-masters.

In this stage of the account, it is clear that the prisoners cannot be completely bound, as they were prior to the release of their fellow prisoner and his return to the cave. They are now able to converse with one another and to make judgments about the identity and sequence of the passing puppets, either directly or with respect to the shadows they cast. Once again, the rank-ordering of these perceptions and the awarding of honors is purely hypothetical (*ei tines autois êsan*: 516c8). The point is not to express a chronological shift in the stage of the cave image, as though the prisoners had been partially detached and had developed speech to describe what they see, thereby moving from one stage of *Unverborgenheit* to another. Instead, Socrates shifts his attention to the futility of judgments, whether perceptual or evaluative, that are rooted within the cave.

But the cave is an image of the process of cognition. The return into the cave results initially in the temporary dimming of the sight of the former prisoner, whose eyes are infected with darkness due to the sudden transition from sunlight to the firelight. If the interval required for visual recovery should be a long one, the prisoners would not only mock the returnee but attempt to kill him. In other words, there is no way for the philosopher to verify discursively the nature of the external world. Each of us must see this for ourselves.

The passage allows a further speculation. The new capacity of the prisoners to speak and to distribute honors may well be due to the escape and return of the free man, or in other words, to the stirring of philosophy. But the mockery and violence to which philosophy is subjected shows us that its influence on the lives of non-philosophers is disruptive, exactly as the main argument of the *Republic* contends. Without fear of anachronism, we can say that Socrates initiates the theme of the danger of philosophy that is an integral element in the western tradition at least through Nietzsche. This theme is rejected in the Enlightenment, especially but not exclusively in France.

We are now in a position to strengthen the previous claim that the disappearance of the puppet-masters is pivotal to our understanding of the allegory of the cave. This disappearance of the masters leaves us with partly freed slaves; even the free man becomes a slave upon his return to the cave, as is indicated by the fact that he sits down again in his old chair (516e4). One could say that the *Republic* as a whole is devoted to a consideration of what would be required to transform the chair into a throne. But the representation of our cognitive faculties as a cave existence to which even philosophers are bound is enough to cast its own shadow of doubt over the interpretation of the dialogue as a serious proposal to resolve the political problem. At the root level, human beings are not concerned with justice, which is never mentioned in the allegory of the cave, but with subservience to *nomos*.

Socrates next makes an explicit connection between the image of the cave and the discussion in Book Six of the Ideas, the Good, and the divided line. The prison home within the cave corresponds to the sphere of sight. The artificial fire within the cave represents the light of the sun that makes vision possible. The journey upward and the viewing of "the upward things" (*tôn anô*) stand jointly for the upward journey of the soul "to the noetic place." So at least Socrates hopes, although only a god knows if it is true (517a8–b7). Let us restate these analogies more explicitly. Prison life refers to the domain of sense perception, but also to the judgments of identity and rank-ordering with respect to the items of genesis. On the divided line, this is called *pistis*. The relevant objects are the artifacts carried round by the puppet-masters. The shadows on the cave wall must refer to the images of *eikasia*. There is no separate representation of the domain of mathematics (*dianoia*), which is assimilated into the viewing of the "upper" objects in the form of the motions of the heavenly bodies. And the sun is of course the symbol of the Idea of the Good.

The comparison between the sun and the Idea of the Good compels Socrates to attribute generative or "productionist" powers to what we can call his first principle (*en te noêtô autê kuria alêtheian kai noun paraschomen*: 517c3–4). I will merely mention, but not insist upon, the fact that Socrates speaks of the sun as an *aitia*, normally translated as "cause," whereas the verb used to designate the activity of the Idea of the Good, *parechomai*, means to supply or furnish. One does not necessarily cause what one furnishes to others. We should also remember in this connection the fact that Socrates refers in Book Ten to god as the "gardener" of the Ideas of artifacts (597d5). These metaphors do not provide us with sufficient evidence to sustain the productionist thesis on the divine or natural level. They certainly do not provide evidence, direct or indirect, for the view, conscious or otherwise, that human cognition produces the Ideas.

In sum, all parts of the image of the cave are now clearly subordinated to the drama of philosophy, including its subnatural origins. This drama illustrates, indirectly and directly, the opposition between politics and philosophy. Justice is never mentioned, nor would there be a place for it on the divided line. Early in the *Republic*, Socrates cites human incompleteness or neediness as the first cause of the city, and says that we would probably observe justice coming into existence together with the city (II. 369a5–b7). In the cave image, the only visible motive for the descent of the philosopher into the city is pity. As to cave existence before the advent of the philosopher, there is no activity by the prisoners and no social intercourse or eros.

The darkness of the Socratic portrait of politics, whether in the cave image or elsewhere in the *Republic*, is a distant ancestor of Heidegger's description of the inauthenticity of everyday life. The difference, of course, between the two doctrines is that Heidegger is no longer concerned with the emergence of the philosopher *per se* into the uncoveredness of truth, but rather with the transformation of everyday into authentic existence. Strange as it may sound, the Heideggerian drama, whether because of or despite its silence about politics, is more "democratic" than its Platonist ancestor, for which authenticity, if I may use that term, is reserved for philosophers.

With respect to metaphysics or ontology, if the Ideas are "grown" or produced by nature, then they must be residents of time, and not simply accessible to us through time, as Socrates puts it in the *Phaedrus*. This problem cannot be evaded by the Platonist because of Plato's catastrophic view of the cosmos. On the other hand, if it is claimed that the Ideas are eternal possibilities that arise with each new ordering of chaos, then, to employ Heidegger's expression, possibility is higher than actuality, and once again, the claim of full presence of that which is always must again be discarded. Differently stated, on this alternative, Plato becomes a modern. But none of these possibilities commits us to a metaphysics of productionism in the precise sense that Heidegger formulates the point in *Platons Lehre von der Wahrheit* and elsewhere.

Whether we take a theoretical or a practical viewpoint, it should be evident by now that the thesis of metaphysical productionism is in contradiction to the thesis of the full presence of the eternal. This result would make nonsense of Heidegger's criticism of Plato. He tries to avoid it by identifying full presence as Plato's conscious doctrine and productionism as its actual but unnoticed consequence. As I have tried to show at some length, the argument is unpersuasive, and it is contradicted by a close analysis of the allegory of the cave, which is the occasion for Heidegger's fullest statement of his position on this point.

To say this is neither to refute Heidegger's own doctrine nor to demonstrate that Platonism is free of serious problems. My point, as I have said throughout these lectures, is that Plato is well aware of the central problem that Heidegger identifies as Platonism. Let me repeat this: Platonism is a problem, not a doctrine. But this is simply to say that philosophy is *unterwegs zur Sprache.*

By way of a conclusion, I want to turn to another aspect of the problem of light and darkness that arises from Plato's separation of good and evil. The difficulty emerges from Socrates' statement that "whoever is going to act prudently in private or public must see [the Idea of the Good]" (517c4–5). One may try to compensate for the absence of any allusions to justice or morality in the image of the cave by invoking the famous Socratic thesis that virtue is knowledge. But what is the connection between sunlight and prudence (*emphronôs praksein*)? Why does seeing an Idea, even the Idea of the Good, tell us how to behave in a particular case?

The function of the Idea of the Good is not to serve as the paradigm or original for good acts, but to furnish the Ideas with illumination. If I perform a good deed, it is not a copy of the Idea of the Good. Goodness, at least on the account presented in the middle books of the *Republic*, and so in the allegory of the cave, plays no practical role whatsoever. Its function is theoretical or ontological. The Good makes existence and cognition possible, but it does not tell us what to do, and certainly not what is morally or politically good and what is evil. This is also evident in Socrates' normal claim that true virtue is knowledge. The philosopher will be an excellent demiurge of "temperance, justice, and the vulgar virtues altogether" (VI. 500d6–9). This is one of the two locations of the actual metaphysics of human production that one finds in Plato; the other, as I have contended, is epistemological.

Since there is no Idea of a contingent human action, the philosopher must produce political and private morality. I know of no serious or extended account in Plato as to how this production is to be effectuated, with the single exception of the everywhere honored principle that philosophy is the highest human good. I suggest that for Plato, an action is finally good or evil depending upon whether it is compatible or not with philosophy. But let us assume for the sake of completeness that the Idea of the Good illuminates everything, including our actions. In this case, it must illuminate vicious and imprudent acts and decisions as well as virtuous and prudent ones. In Book Two (379b15ff), Socrates says that god causes the good only, but not evil. One could say that the presence of the Good illuminates good acts, but how can one say that the absence of the Good illuminates evil acts? This would surely be tantamount to saying that human praxis is a mixture of light and darkness, and that the darkness carries its own light. And this is again a proto-Heideggerian consequence.[4] If virtue, as the Athenian Stranger holds in the *Laws*, is calculation, then vice is miscalculation. Something is missing here: a serious account of evil.

If this objection is sound, then it would seem to follow that the account of the Good is also inadequate. Of course, the image of the cave is concerned almost exclusively with the personal happiness that derives from the vision of the Ideas, but this in itself reinforces the rather Aristotelian tendency to separate theory from practice. The general problem in Plato is that practice takes on the appearance of theory, even as the two are being separated. For example, those who have escaped from the cave are unwilling to "mind the business of human beings" (*ta tôn anthrôpôn prattein*: 517c8–9). "Human business" is presented here as an epistemic or ontological error, not as an ethical or political virtue. Justice (IV. 433a1–b4) requires the philosophers to mind their own business. Justice is for them not political but theoretical, namely, allegiance to the private realm of intelligible beings.

I want to mention one more passage from the conclusion to the story of the cave. I find this passage both odd and suggestive.

---

4   Cf. the discussion of the golden and holy chord that pulls human beings toward virtue in the *Laws*: *Lg.*, I, 644d6ff. The pull is that of calculation (*logismos*).

Socrates says that there are two different causes of visual disturbance: moving from light to darkness and from darkness to light.
If we apply this to the soul, the intelligent man would not laugh
at the victim of the first disturbance but would regard him as
happy because of what he had previously seen, whereas the intelligent man would pity and perhaps laugh at the soul that comes
from darkness to light and is thus unable to see. If he did laugh,
this would be less ridiculous than laughter directed at the soul that
travels from light to darkness (518a1–b4).

There is nothing laughable about moving from light to darkness; this is the direction taken by the released prisoner who
returns to the cave in the attempt to free his former fellow cap-
tives. Socrates says that he should be regarded as blessed because
of his former life, namely, in the light; but he does not say that the
soul should be pitied for having left that life. Let us take this as
corresponding to the nobility of the attempt to rescue one's fellow
human beings from the darkness at the price of re-immersing oneself in the shadows of the cave. But there is no personal happiness
in such a re-immersion. What the philosopher retains are his "rec-
ollections" of life in the light of the Ideas, which he sees through
a glass, darkly.

The confusion connected with the voyage from darkness into
the light deserves pity and is compatible with reasonable, or at
least less ridiculous laughter. I find this more obscure than the first
half of the passage. It would seem to be more reasonable to pity
someone who has returned to the dark than someone who has
arrived in the light. One possibility is that the ascending voyager
is pitiable because he cannot remain in the light but must
inevitably sink back into the cave. Or perhaps darkness remains a
part of human existence even at the peak of our upward journey
into the light. Perhaps a safer interpretation is that the distinction
between greater and less absurdity means here that we are moved
to laugh at both sets of confusion, although it seems clear that the
return to the dark is less laughable. There is something funny
about human existence and this casts its own light into our dark
lives, a light that is entirely foreign to the philosophy of Heidegger.

But we are not gods; wisdom, if it were fully possible, would bring silence, not unquenchable laughter. One last point in this connection: Socrates speaks of pity and laughter, but not of weeping. Laughter is certainly a mark of comedy, whereas pity is associated with tragedy, as Aristotle testifies. The passage just inspected seems to give the palm to laughter over pity, which latter we encountered as the probable cause for the return into the cave. I suggest very tentatively that laughter frees us from politics whereas pity moves us toward it.

In conclusion, the identification of sunlight as firelight in no way introduces a turn from unconcealment to correctness. Instead, it makes a rather Heideggerian point about the shadowy dimension of truth. One could also say that when the shadows are dissipated by sunlight, demotic virtue is transformed into epistemic error. At least Plato had the decency to conceal this troubling consequence. Heidegger did not.

Lecture Five:
Political Construction

In previous lectures I have examined the three main features of Heidegger's interpretation of Plato as the founder of western metaphysics. The first of these three features is what I called the Aristotelianizing of Plato. Heidegger assimilates the Platonic doctrine of the Ideas into Aristotle's account of species-forms, predication, and the science of being qua being. In so doing, he prepares a foundation for his claim that western philosophy is Platonism. The foundation in question is an amalgamation of two imperfectly unified doctrines, namely, noetic intuition and predicative speech.

The main consequence of this disjunction between seeing and talking is as follows. Since there is no predication in the essence, our attention is gradually shifted to the counting and measuring of properties. The entity is then grasped, not as itself, but through its presence to human apprehension as this or that determination. The essence, itself a replacement or concealment of Being, deteriorates further into a *je ne sais quoi*, or the inaccessible *Ding an sich*, and is finally jettisoned altogether in favor of a formal structure of perspectival content, in other words, a human production. Being is concealed, not merely by beings, but by the linguistic transformation of viewpoints into predicates. The initial Platonist impulse to measure correctly the structure of each entity, an impulse that is itself the distant precursor of what Nietzsche calls

the will to power, diverts our attention from truth as the unconcealment or uncoveredness of Being to a conception of truth as the
property of a proposition. Heidegger does not put it in so many
words, but he tacitly argues that the dyad Plato-Aristotle is the
origination of the transformation of philosophy into philosophy
of language. In slightly different terms, it is the replacement of
thinking by philosophy.

Since the language in question is that of properties or predicates of beings rather than of the process of the manifestation of
Being, we lack a criterion by which to rank-order predicates. The
philosophy of Platonic-Aristotelian language, although it originates in the desire to speak the truth about Being as sempiternal
and independent of cognitive construction, is in fact the language
of utilitarianism and extreme subjectivity. In one last expression,
the striving for Idealism terminates in nominalism.

In sum, human beings produce their world through the recon-
struction of eidetic vision as predicative discourse. Knowing is
making. But making is itself directed by the will. From this standpoint, the quarrel between Kant and the empiricists can be seen as
an episode in the struggle to reconcile freedom and autonomy. The
Kantian is free only as bound by rules that he himself has formulated. As has often been stated, however, to pose rules is already
to be beyond them. Let us say that the restlessness of ingenuity
drives autonomy ever closer to anarchy.

By putting the point in this way, one sees the inner link
between theory and practice, or let us say more directly, philosophy and politics. Heidegger tends to express political questions in
world-historical terms; for him politics is a derivative of the history of Being. Plato, on the contrary, tends to express philosophy in
political terms, and for this reason, it would not be amiss to refor-
mulate the quarrel between the two thinkers as one between politics and history. The difference between these two is easily illustrated if one tries to think of Plato or his surrogates as speaking
about the metaphysical destiny of Athens.

On the rare occasions in which Heidegger speaks at any length
about political themes in Plato, he treats them very much as

ontological issues, or let us say as directed toward the two themes of production and *parousia*. He wishes to show Plato as a champion of pure presence who unintentionally, that is, led by the errance of Being, invents the metaphysics of production. Heidegger himself rejects both the intentional and the unintentional versions of Platonism. Nevertheless, he is not as far from these versions as he seems to think. Whereas presence is linked with absence or concealment, it predominates as the epiphany of Being. As to production, it is transferred from human thinking to the "E-vent" of Being.

The problem here is that, at this level of generality, there is nothing to get one's hands on, no way in which to engage with Being. And the problem is exacerbated by speaking scornfully of the attention to beings as utilitarianism or the will to power. Furthermore, what I take the liberty of calling Heidegger's "psychoanalytical" approach to Platonism entirely overlooks the possibility that the patient has a broader view of his own psyche than does the self-appointed therapist. What if the conflict between *parousia* and production is precisely the framework within which we exist? Is it not plausible to regard Platonism as the doctrine that our erotic desire for full presence leads us to produce epistemological and political artifacts to repair, as well as possible, the limitations of noetic vision?

Taken separately, the two doctrines of *parousia* and production seem to oppose rather than to complement one another. And this in turn makes Plato radically less interesting. On my view, the dialectic arises, not as an "either/or" but as both and neither. Perhaps the history of western philosophy can indeed be called "Platonism" or the falling away from Plato's dialectical mastery to the division into two camps of warring disciples. At the same time, it must be admitted that there is no Hegelian "middle" or third term in Platonic dialectic. One finds this middle, if at all, in the myths, not in the so-called arguments of the dialogues.

Heidegger's thesis of productionism becomes more plausible if we consider the many passages in Plato that emphasize the limitations on philosophical intuition. It could then be argued that we produce precisely because of the impossibility of a *parousia*, or at least of one that is fully transmissible into discursive thought (*dianoia*). But rightly or wrongly, Plato never suggests that human production is Nietzschean. It takes a Heideggerian psychoanalyst to demonstrate that the denial of ontological production is in fact its affirmation.

Let me now turn to the main thesis of today's lecture. In the Platonic dialogues, human being is productive in two senses. In the first sense, we produce images of originals but not the originals themselves. The second sense is exhibited in human praxis. I introduce it by reminding you of the seldom mentioned fact that whereas Plato speaks constantly of human nature and the connection between nature and politics, he never says that man is by nature the political animal.

At first thought, one might suppose that such a thesis is intended by Socrates' remark, early in the *Republic* (II. 369b5–c10), that the city originates in our needs, namely, for food, drink, shelter, and sexual reproduction. This observation, however, is entirely insufficient to establish the more general proposition. Strictly speaking, all the mentioned needs could be satisfied, although no doubt with much difficulty, in what modern political philosophers call the state of nature. Socrates himself refers to the result as "the needy city." It is modified by an increase in size, which in turn leads immediately to the adoption of the principle of the division of labor. Very soon thereafter, the city has become luxurious and feverish, and is in obvious need of a physician to purify it (II. 372e3–8). It would seem that no such physician exists in the city prior to Socrates. This claim is also to be found in the *Gorgias*, another dialogue in which philosophy is compared to medicine, and in which Socrates says that he is the only practitioner, or one of the very few, of the true political *technê*.[1]

In other words, contrary to the situation in Aristotle's *Politics*, in which the city grows naturally into its complete, autarchic

---

1   *Grg.* 521d6; cf. 478d6.

form, the Socratic city corrupts us precisely in the process of amending our lack of natural autarchy. In Aristotle, whatever may be the natural end of the highest type of human being, the natural end of the citizen is acquired without philosophy. In Plato, the natural end of the citizen depends entirely upon the rule of the philosopher, who is not present in the city closest to nature, namely, the needy city, which lacks philosophy, to mention only the most important lacuna (II. 372e6–8).

My claim, then, is that the city is for Plato an artificial construction that is required in order to overcome, or better, to control, the natural divisions within the human soul. This is of course in no way to deny that for Plato, human beings are better off in the city than in the state of nature. One has only to mention that philosophy arises exclusively in the city. But it makes no sense to speak of politics as the natural fulfilment of human nature if that fulfilment in turn depends upon compulsion. It may seem anachronistic to some to say that the city is for Plato an artifactual reconstitution of the radically defective work of nature. I myself regard it as the obvious teaching of the two most important political dialogues, the *Republic* and the *Statesman*, to mention only these. The philosopher's political activity, both with respect to the citizen and the city, is regularly presented in the Platonic dialogues as demiurgy. As Socrates says in the *Philebus* (59d10–e3) with respect to the mixture of properties into the life that is good for all human beings: "If someone were to say that the mixture of wisdom and pleasure with one another makes us like demiurges for whom it is necessary to produce something out of something or in something, the verbal likeness would be a fine one."

I want to emphasize that whatever may be true in Aristotle, Plato never presents nature as uniformly friendly or good. We are, by nature, creatures who are prevented from attaining to what nature herself identifies as our greatest happiness. Part of the difficulty in discussing this issue is due to the fact that "nature" (*phusis*) has several senses. Although the point should be well-known, I want to remind you of just a few of its ramifications. Perhaps the most famous of the classical characterizations of nature is

Aristotle's simple but powerful definition: that which happens always or for the most part.[2] This is useful, but unfortunately it overlooks an extremely important question. To say that the sun always rises in the east or that fire burns would be controversial only to a metaphysician or modal logician. Still, even at the level of common sense, these propositions do not convey whether the regularity of nature is good or bad for human beings. To proceed directly to the crux of the matter, the regularity of nature no doubt makes life and sentience possible, but is life good or bad? Aristotle assumes that life in itself is pleasant, but the assertion is hardly immune to debate, nor is pleasure synonymous with goodness.

We touch here upon the famous question of the relation between Aristotle's *Physics* and the *Nicomachean Ethics*. It is still a matter of controversy whether or how much of the theoretical workings of nature must be known in order to understand the nature of praxis. One thing is plain: virtuous deeds do not occur always or for the most part. And the noble is higher than the good; to be good is to be virtuous, but the noble is that at which virtue aims (EN III, 1115b13). Furthermore, life may be pleasant without being good. Could it possibly be true that the best thing for man is not to be born at all, or once born, to die as soon as possible? I am not aware that this question has been definitively settled in the negative. As to the empirical argument that we cling to life, cowardice or fear of death is not a proof that life is good. Again I pass by the intermediate steps. From a theoretical standpoint, the regularity of nature is no doubt highly beneficial. But our estimate of nature from a practical standpoint must be more nuanced. This is forced upon us by the simple recognition that many terrible things happen always or for the most part. But even if this overstates the frequency, no prudent person can deny that natural events are often unreliable guides to our physical and spiritual welfare.

2   [Ed.: See Aristotle's distinction of nature from chance, in *Physics*, II, 8 (198b34–35): "For these things, and all things that are by nature either come to pass as they do always, or for the most part, but none of the things from fortune or chance do."]

In the Platonic dialogues, and perhaps most dramatically in the *Republic*, philosophy is identified as the solution to the problem of the natural sickness of the human race. This solution takes the form of a daydream in which the dramatis personae are said to wish for the rule of philosophy in a properly constructed city. But the city is possible if and only if it possesses leaders who are not merely philosophers but wise in the precise sense that they have mastered dialectic and possess a full vision or Heideggerian *parousia* of the Idea of the Good. Nothing that Socrates says in the *Republic* gives us any confidence that this condition can be fulfilled. Let us, however, assume that it can. In order to rule properly, the philosophers must compel the unwise majority to obey their rule. Very far from furnishing this compulsion, nature must herself be compelled by what might be called militant pharmacological psychiatry.

One can respond to this by holding that nature furnishes us with the problem and the solution, but that in itself does not mitigate the problem or verify the possibility of the solution. Furthermore, Plato's contention is circular, since it would be accepted only by philosophers. And these do not arise always or for the most part. On the contrary, Socrates always emphasizes the rarity of the genuine philosopher. However we look at the matter, one thing seems clear. Philosophers and non-philosophers alike can accomplish very little simply by having recourse to nature. Under the best of assumptions, they must appeal to the right aspect of nature. But nature does not herself explain to us which part is right. It is we who must do the explaining.

The indomitable champion of nature may leave us with the parting assertion that it is she who has produced us as the hermeneutical animal, and this is no doubt true, but it is not very useful, because we must still produce the interpretations. In particular, we must produce an interpretation of Plato. My interpretation begins with the thesis that for Plato, human nature is partly divided against itself. Human being is stamped by what Hegel calls an *"innere Zerrissenheit,"* a tear or rip in our internal fabric which cannot be entirely stitched together by our own efforts. To say this in another way, human nature is partly open; it would cease to be human if it were closed. This tension between openness and closure defines the structure of human activity or politics in the broad sense of the term. It leads to, or is itself the ground of, what I do not hesitate to call a metaphysics of production. We do not grow naturally, nor are the motions of the soul regulated independently of our intentions. On the other hand, we do not simply make ourselves *ex nihilo*. Nature provides us with the problem, and it indicates the elements of the solution. But it is we who must provide the solution.

I mentioned a moment ago the fact that no one in the Platonic dialogues employs the Aristotelian expression that man is by nature a political animal. I would like next to expand on this point, and I start with a broad distinction. The root of the Greek word *phusis* signifies originally both "growth" and "showing forth" or "emergence into the domain of visibility or sunlight." The cosmos is visible but one could not say that it grows; plants grow, and in fact the Greek word for plants is *ta phuta*. In my second lecture, I reminded you that in a striking passage in Book Ten of the *Republic*, Socrates uses the word *phutourgos* or "gardener" to refer to the god who grows the Ideas or paradigms of the entities of genesis. But animals also grow, and thus so too do human beings, whereas one would not normally speak of the "growth" of human artifacts except in a metaphorical sense, or when referring to the results of breeding plants or animals, and so to a modification of living nature. *Phusis* is clearly associated with the notion of life; since this life is not man-made, it is normally attributed to the activity of the gods; and indeed, *phusis* was popularly regarded by the ancients as a goddess. In sum, let us say that the natural is initially and primarily divine life; derivatively, it is everything that is present to human perception and cognition as given to us by the gods. Third, there are deeds and speeches which can be called "natural" even though they are neither simply given nor do they grow forth from the given without human action. Cities do not grow on trees or bushes, but they may be regarded as natural in the sense that human nature can be fulfilled only through political or communal life.

Aristotle's famous assertion, previously cited, that the natural is what occurs always or for the most part, is a kind of secularized version of this broader Greek view. The human changes continually, as does life itself. But the ways in which human things change, like the ways of life and genesis altogether, do not change. This is not enough for an exhaustive account of Aristotle's doctrine of nature, but it will do for our present purposes. "Nature" is orderly change; the ways of change are fixed. This means, of course, that they are not arbitrary or spontaneous, or dependent upon the inscrutable will of the gods. What is fixed in the sense of being regular or orderly is knowable. We can *count* on this order, an expression that brings out very nicely the important role played by mathematics on the one hand and what Aristotle would call the human or political implications of natural order on the other. Nature is not only orderly but it is also authoritative and reliable. As one could also express this, nature is both beautiful and good.

When Aristotle says that man is by nature the political animal, he certainly means to say that human beings must bring cities into existence, but more importantly that the political telos of human nature, while of course depending upon practical intelligence, is accessible to us through practice. I call to your attention a crucial implication of this view. Philosophy, and above all theory, is not necessary for the coming into existence of cities that are adequate, whatever their faults, to the expression of our natural political telos. In other words, closely connected with the thesis that man is by nature the political animal is the Aristotelian tripartition of theory, practice, and production. The perfection of theory, or the *bios theoretikos*, is not the same as the perfection of practice or the *bios praktikos*. It is not merely that cities come into existence without philosophers; what is also the case is that the perfection of the political component of human nature does not depend upon philosophy. It is therefore also true that for Aristotle, the satisfaction of the political telos does not depend upon the achievement of some extreme, unnatural form of perfection. This constellation of doctrines is quite foreign to, and was certainly intended as a criticism of, Plato.

Whereas Plato of course speaks of "the nature" of the city, just as he does of the nature of man, he does so to designate its power or essence: the way in which it must be, in order to fulfil the function of a city. The city is not, however, "natural" in the Aristotelian sense that it is the orderly consequence of man's political nature. As noted previously, Socrates speaks on more than one occasion of human beings as sick by nature, as having disordered souls that require philosophical therapy or psychiatry, as incapable of living just or good lives unless they are healed or governed by philosopher-kings. For this reason his usual account of the city is that of an artifact. This is evident in the terminology of the *Republic* and in the central paradigm of the *Statesman*, namely, weaving, to mention only the two most authoritative sources for Plato's political views. Aristotle would no doubt agree with Plato's view of the defects of human nature, but not at all with the diagnosis of a sickness that can be cured only by a combination of violence and philosophy. Aristotle's *Ethics* and *Politics* are intended as expressions of political excellence that is accessible by nature. Plato's *Republic*, even if we do not take it literally as a prescription for actual political revolution, nevertheless (and even more on this supposition) expresses the impossibility of attaining to political excellence by what Aristotle would call natural means.

In the *Gorgias*, Socrates speaks of justice as the medicine of the soul (478d6–7). Whereas health is the order of the body, justice and temperance are the order of the soul (504c5–d4). In an earlier passage, Gorgias, the great rhetorician, describes how his brother, a physician, engaged him to persuade a patient to take a bitter medicine (456b1ff). Socrates subsequently says that the art of rhetoric in the usual sense stands to medicine as does the art of the pastry chef to that of the gymnastics trainer (465c1ff). But Socrates claims to be virtually the only Athenian who practices the true art of politics, and in so doing, compares himself to a physician (521d6ff, e3ff). The genuine art of politics is in other words the medicine of the soul; philosophy is required to heal injustice.

Art is required in order to rectify the natural disorder of the human being. This series of passages should be connected to the discussion of genuine or philosophical rhetoric in the *Phaedrus*, where Socrates refers to rhetoric as the medicine of the soul (270b1–c2). The rhetoric of Gorgias is akin to that of the pastry cook, but this does not mean that rhetoric is superfluous to politics. What we require is the rhetoric of Socrates or Plato himself, or genuine rather than specious psychiatry.

The intrinsic sickness or psychic disorder of the human being is also central to the political discussion in the *Republic*. What Socrates calls the "true" and "healthy" city is almost immediately rejected because of Glaucon's complaint that its citizens are restricted to a vegetarian diet and have no couches on which to recline while eating (372e6–8). Socrates does not mention it, but we may note that in this true city, which is fit for pigs but not human beings, there is no philosophy. Socrates is forced to start again in the construction of what will be called the just or "beautiful" city (VII. 527c2) in which philosophers rule. Socrates calls this city "luxurious" (*truphôsan*: II. 372e3) and "fevered" (*phlegmainousan*: e6–8). The natural disorder or sickness of the human soul is thus represented by Glaucon, the extremely erotic youth (III. 403a4–5; V. 474d4) who is also very courageous (II. 357a3). Glaucon is the interlocutor in the most philosophical passages of the dialogue and it is he who encourages Socrates to speak about topics which the philosopher is reluctant to discuss, including the noble lie (III. 414c11) and the nature of the good (VI. 509c3–6).

Glaucon's erotic nature is a perfect image of the sickness intrinsic to the human being. On the one hand, eros is an essential component of the philosophical nature, as we know not only from the *Symposium* and *Phaedrus* but also from the discussion of the philosopher in the *Republic*.[3] On the other hand, the *Republic* makes explicit the political danger of eros by identifying it as a

---

3   For a detailed treatment of this point, see my article "The Role of Eros in Plato's *Republic*," reprinted in *The Quarrel between Philosophy and Poetry: Studies in Ancient Thought* (New York, Routledge, 1988), 102–118.

tyrant and madman that drives out the useful desires such as shame and temperance (573b1–4). Eros *turannos* (573b6–7) is obviously unjust, and hence constitutes the sickness of the soul. The intrinsic ambiguity of eros is not overcome by the claim that the philosophical eros differs in nature from that of the body; this is not correct. As is obvious throughout the dialogues, the human eros must be transformed or deflected from its corporeal objects to a desire for the Platonic Ideas; but it is the same eros in all cases. In the *Symposium*, it is not Socrates who distinguishes between a noble and a base eros but the refined pederast Pausanias. That the philosopher, as hyper-erotic and even manic, is an extremely dangerous type, quite unstable in his youth, is made plain in the *Republic* at VI.491e1ff, where Socrates explains how the best natures are the most harmed by a bad education, and that unless he is saved by good luck, even the well-educated philosopher will be destroyed by the wrong soil and nurture.

The philosopher is a physician of the soul (cf. VI. 489c1) who must moderate or shape the fundamentally erotic nature of the human being by an elaborate political rhetoric that features the telling of medicinal lies (II. 382c6ff; III. 389b2ff, 414b8ff; V. 459c2–d1) and the comprehensive regulation of education from the cradle to the grave in the case of the guardians. This of course raises the question of who will properly train the potential philosophers. Socrates' reply is explicit if not entirely unambiguous. The fate of the potential philosopher depends upon good luck, as for example in his own case, namely, the *daimonion* or demonic voice that saved him from his own divided nature. As for his successors, they will be trained by Socrates, or rather by Plato, who assumes the prototypical figure of the philosophical prophet and lawgiver.

I note that at III. 399e5–7, Socrates claims that the musical and gymnastic education they have designed amounts to a purging of the luxury of the city. He does not say that it has purged the fevers of the city. But we do not need to argue from silence. The elaborate steps taken to control sexual reproduction among the guardians, including rigged lotteries to select mates, direct lies, and the destruction of offspring of uneugenic intercourse (V. 459a1–460c5) will eventually fail, thus leading to the destruction of the city (VIII. 546a2ff). But even while the city exists, it will contain injustice. Socrates says (III. 410a2–4) that the physicians of this city will put to death those who are sick in the soul. More dramatically still, the largest class in the city, consisting of workers of all kinds, is not subjected to the education, restrictions on breeding, or supervision of occupations that stamp the souls of the guardians. It is obvious that the largest portion of the city is thus characterized by an intrinsic or natural injustice that cannot be removed by philosophy but only regulated by the police. Nor should one forget the philosophers themselves, who would prefer to philosophize but who are compelled to rule. It would take too long to analyze this complex and controversial issue; suffice it to say that there is legitimate reason for supposing that, in compelling them to choose an inferior over a superior life, the city is doing an injustice to its best citizens. Finally, I remind you that the first act of the philosopher kings will be to send everyone over the age of ten into the countryside (VII. 540e5), an obvious euphemism for something very close to what is today called "ethnic cleansing."

It is true that, according to Socrates, the just city has been built "in accord with nature" (IV. 428e9). But it is equally true that the human being is divided against itself by nature, as is most obvious from the ambiguity of eros, the principle of philosophy and tyranny. Plato's point is no different from that of Machiavelli in the *Prince*: justice depends upon initial injustice; nor will the latter ever be eradicated from human affairs. It can only be controlled by medicinal lies, rhetoric, and purges and these are to be administered by the most virtuous and hence the most just citizens. There is no equivalent in Plato to the Stoic doctrine of living harmoniously in accord with nature, a doctrine that is so castigated by Nietzsche. Parenthetically, I note that in the Romantic period, of which the twentieth century, for better and for worse, is a distorted continuation, there comes into view a doctrine of living in accord with nature understood as the countryside in opposition to the city. I suppose that Rousseau is as responsible for this doctrine as anyone; it is clear, however, that this is not a political but an anti-political teaching, and that it too points to the underlying notion of a divided human nature. This of course is not the Platonic view; in the *Phaedrus*, Socrates makes it clear that philosophy belongs to the city rather than to the countryside or the natural landscape, to mention only the decisive point. If it is true in a general sense that Plato accepts the view of human being as by nature political, the fact remains that human nature is divided against itself. What Socrates calls "the healthy and just character" of the philosophical nature, which hates the lie in the soul and avoids the chorus of evils that follow the many non-philosophers (VI. 490b9–c6), must regulate the erotic madness of the many by its own erotic madness. The tyranny of intemperance in the many will be transformed into the tyranny of sobriety in the few.

In sum: according to Plato, the human being must be modified by philosophical *technê*, and this includes philosophical rhetoric; the human being is sick by nature and must be healed by philosophical psychiatry, in order to live in a properly constructed city. The citizen is a work of art, not of course a perfect work of art but one in which the inner contradiction of human nature can be contained within a harmony induced by the right kind of *paideia* for as long as possible. I can now refine my thesis about Plato as follows. The city as such is natural in the sense that it comes into existence because the individual human being is not autarchic but has need of others. But there is no perfection of praxis or political virtue by nature, as there is for Aristotle. In the extreme formulation of Socrates at *Republic* VI. 500d4–9, the philosopher will be a good demiurge, i.e., artisan, "of temperance, justice, and all of demotic virtue." Temperance and justice are the key political virtues, but they are part of demotic or vulgar virtue, which is to say that they are fashioned by political demiurges, and in the wished-for case, by the philosophical demiurge.

I believe we can now see why it is a complete mistake to take one's bearings by the expulsion of the mimetic poets in attempting to understand Plato's *Republic*. The mimetic poets are expelled because they are to be replaced by the philosopher-kings, not because poetry is to be replaced by mathematics or dialectic. This is why we cannot take literally or narrowly Socrates' remarks to the effect that he and his interlocutors are not poets but *oikistai poleôs*, "builders of the city" (II. 378e7–379a1). They are indeed *builders*; as such, they must abstain from all other demiurgic arts and be *dêmiourgous eleutherias tês poleôs*, "demiurges of the city's freedom" (III. 395b8–c1). That this art is not to be carried through in meter or verse is irrelevant (see III. 393d8); it is a poetic or productive art; the name "demiurge" is in one sense of course metaphorical, but the point of the metaphor is to make explicit the constructive nature of the art of philosophical politics.

So much for the terminology of the *Republic*, examples of which could easily be multiplied to confirm the points I have made. I turn now to the *Statesman*, a dialogue of Plato's later years, and one in which the Eleatic Stranger replaces Socrates as the main interlocutor. I can only mention here that one meaning of this shift is to indicate the more theoretical or as we would say "abstract" nature of the treatment of politics in the *Statesman* as compared with that in the *Republic*. The very success of the *Republic*, which is due to its resemblance to a kind of comprehensive novel in the style of Tolstoy, has prevented many readers from noticing that it is indeed a philosophical novel, even a fairy tale about the relation between philosophy and politics. We have been deluded on the one hand by Socrates' criticism of mimetic poetry, and on the other by the magic of Plato's mimetic poetry, and so failed to notice that, with all of its discussion of the Ideas, the Good, and the role of mathematics in a philosophical education, the *Republic* is a poetical presentation of the problem of philosophical politics.

However this may be, the Eleatic Stranger makes entirely prosaic the Socratic view of politics as demiurgic, rhetorical, or constructive. The central paradigm, or as we would say today, model, of the art of politics is the art of weaving.[4] Weaving makes

---

4   For details, see my *Plato's Statesman: The Web of Politics* (New Haven: Yale University Press, 1995).

artificial products like curtains, blankets, and cloaks in order to protect the body from the painful and destructive effects of nature. As the Stranger formulates his final definition of the art of politics, the statesman "rules all of the arts and cares for the laws and everything in the city and weaves them all together most effectively" (305e2–6). The statesman is not a creator *ex nihilo*. Just as the weaver is furnished with wool by nature, so the statesman is furnished by nature with the fundamental materials of the city, namely, two types of human natures (306e9ff), one courageous and sharp, the other moderate and gentle. These two human types are in a certain manner enemies; a condition of political discord (*stasis*) exists between them. In other words, nature furnishes the philosopher-statesman with discordant materials and leaves it to him to harmonize them or weave them together into a city, which is artificial in the fundamental sense that it is not supplied by nature, and in particular not by our *political* nature. We are by nature enemies, and our cities, unless respun by the philosophical weaver, are in the natural condition of revolution. As a consideration of the subsequent description of political weaving would show, the philosopher stands to the city as does the divine artificer of the *Timaeus* to the cosmos. It should also be mentioned that from 293b1 almost to the end of the dialogue, the Stranger regularly compares politics with medicine.

The conclusion about weaving together different natures does not deviate substantially from that of the *Republic* (see for example III. 410d1ff; the philosophers must harmonize the hard and the soft natures by a judicious mixture of gymnastics and music), but it does bring out certain ambiguities that are left undiscussed and even unmentioned in the earlier, Socratic presentation. I will give just one example. According to the Stranger, those who are by nature gentle or moderate try to live in an orderly and quiet way, *ta sphetera autôn prattontes*, "tending to their own affairs" or "minding their own business" (307c9–e4). This is of course almost literally the definition of justice given by Socrates in the *Republic* (III. 433a1–b4). Socrates means that each of us ought to perform the basic type of work for which we are best suited, namely, philosophy, soldiering, or the arts and crafts, farming, and physical labor. But this is a matter of justice, and so of politics, not of personal happiness. Our goal is not to make even the guardians happy, although Socrates assures us that they will be, but rather to make the city as happy as possible (III. 419a1ff).

Apart from the absurdity of a happy city, and indeed one in which happiness is so variously enacted as in the *Republic*, it is clear that in the crucial case, that of the guardians, Socrates intends "one's own" to be interpreted as strictly as possible to mean "the city." In the *Statesman*, on the other hand, "one's own" means whatever makes one personally content or happy. To recur to a previous point, let us assume that it is just in the beautiful city for philosophers to be compelled to rule rather than to devote themselves to the study of philosophy in their private capacities. In order to make this assumption, we must also assume that by shifting from that at which they are best, and which is the best life in itself, namely, philosophy, to something at which they may excel but which is neither best in itself nor does it constitute their personal happiness, the philosopher-kings exemplify justice, or minding their own business, by not minding their own business but that of everyone else, and so by exercising *polupragmosunê* or injustice.

Even on the basis of these assumptions, it remains the case that justice and happiness are not entirely compatible. Perhaps even more important, however, from a political standpoint, is the fact that the correct political interpretation of "minding one's own business" requires violence to be effected upon the sense of "one's own." The problem was clear in the *Republic* as early as Book II, 375a2ff. The guardians must be both sharp or courageous, and so cruel to enemies, but also gentle to friends. In order to support his contention that the mixture of these attributes is not contrary to nature, Socrates cites the example of the noble hound who barks at strangers and is gentle to friends. The choice of a beast as the paradigm of human nature is obviously a joke, not to mention a circular one, since the political attributes of dogs have undoubtedly been inculcated into them by generations of breeding and training. But it is in any case silently rejected by the subsequent reliance upon the education of body and soul in order to produce by art what nature herself cannot supply.

It makes no difference that the best interests of the courageous and the moderate alike are served by a harmonious city. The main point is that no such city can arise, or if it arises, last for more than a short interval, unless it has been woven together by the royal art of the statesman. I repeat: the materials are furnished by nature, but the city is not. Human beings are by nature enemies, very much as Thomas Hobbes, the ostensible founder of modern political philosophy, who was of course only following Machiavelli, said that they are. To come back to the *Statesman*, the Stranger tells us that the two kinds of human natures "are always marked by the greatest enmity and stasis with respect to each other" and so that "not the least parts of virtue differ from each other by nature, as do the deeds of those who possess them" (308b2–8). This passage is important because it differs from the usual Socratic contention that the virtues are one. The difference can be partly removed by noting that Socrates regards virtue as knowledge; in other words, all virtues other than wisdom are demotic or not genuine virtues. As he says in the *Republic*, at VII. 518d9–e3, the so-called virtues, namely, those other than intelligence (*phronesis*), are close to those of the body and are produced by habituation and exercise. But that does not alter the political situation. Neither nature nor political prudence in the usual or non-philosophical sense will overcome this natural split between human kinds. That task can be performed by the philosopher alone, the royal weaver, as we may call him.

One has to underline in red the important conclusion that for Plato there is no such thing as political virtue in the Aristotelian sense. There is no practical virtue as distinguished from theoretical and productive virtue. On the contrary, there are only theory and production; this is the principle in accord with which the arts and sciences are regularly classified in the Platonic dialogues. And it remains a deep question in Plato, seldom noticed but nevertheless of crucial importance, whether politics is a theoretical or a practical art. In the division of the arts in the *Statesman*, the interlocutors begin by classifying the statesman under the epistemonic men, i.e., those who are knowers rather than makers (258e4ff). But the dialogue culminates in a comparison of the statesman to the weaver or maker, and it is this paradigm that is followed subsequently. I cannot go into the extraordinary intricacy of the intermediate steps, which I dissect in my book on the *Statesman*, but the result is plain. Just as diaeresis is constructive in the modern sense of the term because it makes new concepts like that of the art of tending horned herd-animals, or whatever else is necessary to the intentions of the diaeretician, so too politics is not pure gnosis but is at the same time construction. The very least one could say (in the terminology of the *Statesman*) is that politics is the art of commanding for the sake of a genesis. We cannot simply say that the city requires guardians who exhibit the paradigm of the noble hound; we must construct a new type of human being by devising a sound set of procedures which are furnished not by political prudence but by the madness of philosophy.

The *Statesman* is a maddeningly obscure as well as a perversely amusing dialogue. It forces us to consider the political analogues of carding and combing wool, as well as of arts like that of the fuller, the mender, and the washer of clothing. But the central image is not difficult to decipher. The statesman is neither a shepherd of a herd nor a captain of the ship of state – two metaphors for the royal art of politics that are initially suggested and then rejected or radically modified. Herds are not cities, nor are their members human beings; the captain does not participate in the building of his ship nor is he responsible for the deeds performed by his passengers when they reach their destination. Of the many paradigms entertained in the *Statesman*, perhaps that of the architect comes closest to the central figure of the weaver. Both make clear the need to construct artifacts for the protection of the human race against nature. In this sense there is a genuine anticipation of the theme of the modern

Enlightenment, although self-defense rather than mastery is the central issue.

I said a while ago that the *Statesman* is more theoretical than the *Republic*. The Stranger makes it clear that the purpose of his conversation about politics is not political but is rather intended to make his pupils "more dialectical" (*dialektikoteros*) about everything. The stated purpose of the *Republic*, on the other hand, is to persuade Glaucon and Adeimantus that the just life is intrinsically more choiceworthy than the unjust life. Everything said in this dialogue is accommodated to the understanding and desires of his youthful interlocutors, including the treatment of topics like the Ideas and the Good (VI. 504b1–8, 509c3f). Whereas dialectic is the peak of education within the guardian class of the just city (VII. 534e2), it can only be described metaphorically, in images like that of the sun, to Glaucon and his companions. The Stranger, on the other hand, is training in the first instance young mathematicians; he engages in extended exercises of diaeresis if not in Socratic dialectic, and he discusses at some length such topics as paradigms and measurement. Throughout this dialogue, the emphasis is upon theoretical construction, another example of how the *Statesman* is surprisingly modern in its themes, despite the archaic form of its rhetoric. I do not want to overstate this point, but it is nevertheless true to a considerable extent that the *Republic* emphasizes the link between mathematics and the eternal, whereas the *Statesman* emphasizes concept-construction or more generally, the constructive nature of the method of diaeresis and conceptual analysis.

One could also say that poetry dominates the presentation of eternity in the *Republic*, whereas in the *Statesman*, eternity is represented predominantly if not always as changing, and in particular in the great myth of the reversed cosmos. It would be very foolish to attempt to draw general inferences about Plato's doctrines from these brief comparisons of the two dialogues, or for that matter from the more extended sample of evidence contained in my lecture as a whole. I have hoped to show, or at least to make plausible, the claim that Plato views human being as divided in nature and hence as by nature incomplete, *das noch nicht fest-gestellte Tier*, as Nietzsche expresses a related thought.[5] This is the teaching of the Greek tragedians, and this is the most important link between Nietzsche's psychology and that of Plato. In this connection, I add that whatever one may think of Nietzsche's criticism of Socrates and his ostensibly anti-dramatic rationalism, Nietzsche does not identify Socrates with Plato as do so many less perceptive classicists.

I want to take up one last point. Since this is in effect my peroration, I ask you to indulge a very general reflection. The fundamental tension in Platonism is that of the possibility of constructing a political artifact in the light of eternal order. I have tacitly suggested that Plato shows us in the two quite different images of the *Republic* and the *Statesman* the same underlying need to create by poetry and philosophical rhetoric a city that serves to protect human beings against themselves as well as the hostile characteristics of the cosmos. Whatever may be the ontological truth about the Platonic Ideas, they serve what most of us would call a "conservative" political function, and the same is finally true of the various technical exercises of the Eleatic Stranger.

I hesitate to use the term "conservative" because I do not wish to invoke contemporary political ideologies. I use it to designate the posture of self-defense against nature. Aristotle, who is as sober as Plato is mad, comes much closer to the Stoic notion of living in accord with nature, but only, I think, at the price of suppressing the problems that are so vividly, if at the same time ambiguously, presented in the Platonic dialogues. I sometimes wonder whether the doctrine that man is by nature the political animal is not Aristotle's noble lie, and whether his soothing rhetoric is not intended to function as the genuine political medicine that replaces and corrects the damage instilled by Plato's excessively daring pharmaceutical recipes.

---

5   [Ed.: In his spoken remarks, Prof. Rosen attributes this statement to Zarathustra. I have corrected it to Nietzsche since the phrase appears in *Beyond Good and Evil*, aph. 62.]

It is a long story but it would be very rewarding to make a detailed study of why the modern scientific and by extension political revolution begins under the flag of Plato rather than Aristotle. I have tried to tell a part of that story today by bringing out a side to Plato that is seldom given its due, namely, his political constructivism and his perception of the uneasy residence of human being within a nature that is hostile as much as it is friendly to our healthy existence. Whereas Aristotle may finally be a better political poet than Plato, I believe that we have more to learn from Plato at this juncture of late modernity (late at least for us). Under no circumstances would I wish to be understood as suggesting that part of what we need to learn is how to construct a healthy city, if this is taken to mean an endorsement of the beautiful city of the *Republic*, which is neither beautiful nor a genuine city on its own criterion of unity.

I conclude with a brief remark concerning the metaphysics of production. The construction of the city does not take place in the light of *parousia*, or the full presence of the Ideas to the eye of the intellect. On the contrary, it takes place in the mixture of presence and absence, by which I refer to the disjunction within the soul that not only prevents us from living in accord with nature but makes such an accord impossible for living and sentient beings like ourselves. It thus turns out that on Platonic principles, we must participate in the production of the city as an expression of human being. Indeed, such a participation is what it means to live a human life. Unfortunately, we are ill-equipped for the task of such a life, as is entirely evident to those who are awake, thanks to the need of the philosopher to use extreme compulsion. We are free to live defective lives, but we must be forced to live in accord with nature. And this means that it is not simply nature to which we must accommodate ourselves but to our own productive activity as well.

Lecture Six:
The Production of Ideas

Thus far I have argued that Heidegger is mistaken in his formulation of the presence of a doctrine of the production of the Platonic Ideas. But this does not mean that the doctrine of production is absent from Platonism. A productive element is to be found in Plato's account of the process of cognition, or what is today called "epistemology," as well as in the domain of praxis or politics. In the language of the *Republic*, we manufacture images of epistemic originals, but not the originals themselves. On the other hand, Socrates does say that the Idea of the Good is the cause of the being of the other Ideas. Depending upon what we make of statements like this, it seems possible to identify a productive component in the domain of the Ideas themselves. But this is not the same as to attribute the production of Ideas to human beings.

One may say that the crucial point in Platonism is the legitimacy of the distinction between the production of knowledge and the discovery of what regulates this production. Much the same situation obtains within Heidegger's own thought. I refer to the distinction between beings and Being. The central point of Heidegger's critique of Platonism is to preserve the encounter with the manifestation of Being from infection by human constructive activity. On this point, Heidegger is himself a Platonist, and he is guilty of the same unawareness of the implication of his effort that he attributes to Plato.

The serious question, however, is not that of textual interpretation. It is rather whether philosophy can be preserved from the virtual axiom of modern thought that we know only what we make. This question, in other words, is not captured in the discussion of a quarrel between genuine philosophical thinking and technology. Technology is itself one of the two principal weapons of poetry in its quarrel with philosophy, the other weapon being rhetoric. In another series of lectures, this comment could be spelled out at the length it deserves. Here I can only mention that poetry is a force of emancipation or freedom of the will that animates modern technology, which is incapable of articulating its own ideology.

My own view is that this issue cannot be decided by logical argumentation. As Heidegger himself remarked on more than one occasion, a problem that can be resolved is not a genuine philosophical problem. This does not mean that arguments are irrelevant, but only that they are frequently selected on the basis of insights or pre-theoretical convictions about how things must be, even if we cannot succeed in a full demonstration of the veracity of those convictions. What Plato calls "recollection" and Heidegger "pre-ontological understanding" have something essential to do with this point.

One of the most illuminating examples of the nature of philosophical problems is the ongoing controversy among logicians and mathematicians about whether numbers, sets, relations, and so on exist or are produced by the practitioners of the techniques of formalism. It is obvious that logic and mathematics can be done at the highest technical level regardless of whether one is a Platonist or an anti-Platonist. The choice here is not simply between two kinds of mathematics, but rather between two philosophical interpretations of the nature of mathematics. Once the philosophical question has been answered, there are of course consequences for what counts as legitimate mathematical procedure. But it would be difficult to say that these consequences lead to better or worse mathematical reasoning. What counts as better or worse here is finally dependent upon one's philosophical views, not on differences in technique. It is therefore naive to assume that the nature of Platonic Ideas can be established or decisively clarified by the use of elaborate technical machinery. The first step here would be to establish the philosophical implications of the machinery itself.

Fundamental philosophical problems are then open to more than one technical approach, and which approach we choose is at least partly determined by what we regard as sensible. But this general difficulty casts its shadow across all philosophical theories. To take a difficulty that is specific to the present series of lectures, we cannot say whether Ideas are produced until we know what they are. But there is no canonical statement of the doctrine of Ideas in the Platonic dialogues. Sometimes the main interlocutor speaks as though Ideas are the unique originals of which generated particulars are images, and sometimes he speaks as though we have direct access to Ideas. I note the suggestive fact that when Socrates is the main interlocutor, he usually makes a decent attempt to derive the plausibility of the existence of Ideas from an analysis of ordinary experience. Important examples are the *Republic* and the *Phaedo*. But in dialogues like the *Philebus*, in which Socrates is again the main speaker, and the *Sophist*, in which he is virtually silent, there is much talk of the division and collection of things in accordance with kinds, but no detailed description of a method for identifying Ideas that could actually be followed in a step-by-step manner. And the same is true of the art of dialectic itself as described in the *Republic*.

This difficulty is connected to the further embarrassment that it is not at all clear how to determine the precise domain of generated particulars to which Ideas correspond. The so-called "greatest genera" of the *Sophist* have nothing in common with Ideas of cows or horses (or what Aristotle calls separate substances), and neither of these is anything like formal relations, or moral attributes. And this is to say nothing of the vexed question whether there are Ideas of human artifacts like beds and tables. In the face of so much confusion and diversity, one scarcely knows how to go about investigating Platonism, let alone defending it.

Thus far in this series of lectures, I have taken my bearings by Heideggerian interpretations of particular Platonic texts, and tried to show that these interpretations are incomplete, implausible, or insufficiently precise. Today, my intention is different. By way of a conclusion to the entire series, I want to consider the main points of traditional Platonism, and to suggest some modifications that are required, not simply to meet Heidegger's objections, but to make Platonism defensible. Some of you may regard my modifications as a rejection of Platonism. But I make no claim here to philological orthodoxy. My goal is not to rescue traditional Platonism from the mephitic atmosphere of the Schwarzwald. It is rather to indicate the intellectual work that these texts demand of us in the attempt to determine the truth.

I shall suggest three principles, or what I call axioms, of "Platonism" that underlie the doctrine of Ideas. By way of a prelude, let me remark that in my opinion, Heidegger is right to see the fundamental issue of Platonism in the quarrel between discovery and production. Whether discovery can preserve its independence from, and priority over production, depends upon the aforementioned principles. If the principles require modification, this is not necessarily because Platonism is mistaken in its central adherence to discovery, but, as I believe is the case, it may be that the modifications are necessary to preserve Platonism itself.

Let us take our bearings by what Socrates calls in the *Republic* "our usual procedure" of establishing a one over many. That is, we collect together those particular items of everyday life which are all instances of the same family or nature. No argument is presented to justify our ability to divide and collect in accordance with kinds. The sameness of kind is directly accessible by inspection of the looks and behavior of the items themselves. Mistakes in identification are corrected by taking another look at the item in question.

This very preliminary account already provides the anti-Platonist with an objection. Have I not in effect granted that the discovery of sameness is itself a function of experience and that it cannot be established with the precision required for the presence of an Idea? But the point here is that even to suppose that two items are of the same kind is already to make use of what is perhaps the most important axiom of Platonism. It is an empirical question whether the items are indeed of the same kind, but it is a matter of principle that to be is to be something or another of such and such a kind. We could conceivably mistake a cow for a horse, in which case our collection of horses would erroneously include some cows. But this empirical error would not change the kind or Idea of horses into the Idea of cows.

In other words, it is false or seriously incomplete to say that we arrive at the notion of a class or kind by inspecting a large number of individuals and finally drawing the inductive conclusion that they are all, say, cows. We could not "inspect" a single item if it were not already identifiable and re-identifiable as an item of this sort. This is a slight oversimplification, since explicit identifications of kind are surely embedded in the heterogeneity of experience, namely, the fact that experience consists from the outset of heterogeneity, that is, a multiplicity of items that can be sorted out into collections of a definite kind. After all, to identify is also to differentiate, and this is made possible by the identities of the items being distinguished. This is how we arrive at a one over many.

I believe that this helps us to understand Plato's apparently incredible doctrine of recollection. It would be circular to claim that we identify Ideas by discerning the sameness of kind in particular individuals, whereas we identify the kind of individual by reference to its Idea. If the identification is attributed to the vision of the Ideas in a previous existence, we still have to explain how the Idea was perceived in that incarnation, and this leads to an infinite regress. The simplest alternative is to say that the perception of the sameness in kind between two or more individuals is itself the apprehension of the Platonic Idea. "Recollection" thus refers to the realization that this is so. What precisely this means is a question that will occupy us throughout the balance of my lecture.

It is then of great importance to Platonism that misidentification is as much dependent upon kinds as is identification. To misidentify is to place something in the wrong kind, and this is possible only because we recognize that things exemplify kinds. That is, we identify and correct our mistakes by noticing that what seemed to be a horse is in fact a cow, not that there is no difference between horses and cows. Human existence as a whole is a process of dividing and collecting according to kind, and this in turn is because to be is to be something of such and such a kind.

The first axiom of Platonism is then the definiteness of things. A corollary to this axiom is that we cannot speak of Being in the Heideggerian sense except by contrast with speech about beings in the Platonist sense. But even farther, language is itself "Platonist" or thing-oriented, as is obvious from Heidegger's efforts to find a way of "bespeaking" Being. To refer to Being, for example, as a round dance is to be as dependent upon reification as to speak of Ideas and essences. Even the speech that asserts the difference between predicates and Being is inevitably predicational discourse. Either Being has properties or it does not. If it does, then we must employ predication and reification in attempting to explain it. If it does not, then we must keep silent.

Not at all obvious is the second axiom of Platonism, namely, that the kind or Idea, say of the cow, is separate from the changes undergone by the things of that kind, namely, cows. This axiom is necessary because of Plato's conception of knowledge as unchanging and indubitable. There is accordingly no genuine knowledge (*epistêmê*) of items of the domain of genesis, but at best correct opinion or belief (*orthê doksa*). Genuine knowledge, where it is possible at all, can only be of the Idea, that is, of the monad or unity that constitutes the "one" in a one over many. This corresponds to Heidegger's contention that for Plato, truth is the full presence of what is always and which presents itself as always what it fully is.

If the axiom of separation is rejected, then it is difficult if not impossible to prevent the contamination of the Idea by the uncertainty of genesis. On the other hand, if the axiom is accepted, it becomes equally difficult to explain how we discover the Idea at all, or if we do so, what role it plays in the existence and intelligibility of its empirical instances. From the outset, it looks as though the axiom must be modified in such a way as to prevent both contamination and complete detachment.

Axiom 2 raises the technical question of the relation between the one and the many that it unifies. It is this point that Aristotle elaborated into the *chôrismos* problem. How can the Idea be (what Aristotle calls) the essence of a given item if it is separated from that item? Must there not be a second form that expresses what is common to the item and its separate instantiation? And does this not lead to the infinite regression of the so-called "third man" problem?

Axiom 2 seems to sustain the following thesis. If the Idea cannot be distinguished from its generated instance, then we cannot possess a full and complete intuition of what it genuinely is. There must be a difference between Idea and instance that is not a full separation. In the canonical terminology, the instance "participates" in the Idea. But how do we know this? Since Ideas are inferred from the sameness of kind of a collection of sensed particulars, it would be mistaken to hold that the Idea reveals itself, wholly or partially, in a spontaneous manner, entirely independent of sense perception. The one *over* many is the one or unity *of* the many. We see or "intuit" the Idea by so to speak repairing the damage that is evident in the perceptual content of our cognition of multiple items. The justification for this step is that the changing aspects of, say, a cow, cannot in themselves be the stable formal properties that we know are necessary for things to possess an identity, and thereby to be identifiable as things of such-and-such a kind.

In sum, Ideas are continuously functioning in the domain of genesis, but it requires an act of retrospective analysis ("recollection") to become aware of them. Still more succinctly, we first cognize and then understand that and how we are doing so. This has a very important consequence. The different degrees of completeness that mark our grasp of Ideas at any particular time are quite distinct from the fullness of the present Idea. A blurred grasp of, say, a cow does not mean that the Idea of the cow is blurred. But neither does a blurred vision of the Idea of the cow entail the incomplete nature of that Idea.

In other words, there is no such thing as a partial Idea. Ideas do not have parts, although each "uncuttable atom" may commune or associate with other such atoms. The atom is uncuttable in much the same sense that there is no before and after, i.e., no owner and property, in the interior of an Aristotelian essence. If we could separate a formal structure into properties, then we would be dealing with an incompletely divided community of Ideas. But if I see that each member of a given multiplicity is of the same kind as every other member, then I have seen the full Idea that corresponds to every instance of that kind. In short, an Idea is not a complex structure of separable elements, although it may participate as an atom in such a structure. The Idea is seen whole or not at all. But for that reason it cannot be like the perception of empirical cows or horses.

This raises a famous paradox that is discussed in the *Theaetetus*, and in our day by Wittgenstein. If Ideas (or formal atoms) are the last step of formal analysis, then they must each be perfectly simple, that is, have no heterogeneous parts. But in this case, they cannot be perceived, and so they all collapse into an Eleatic monad. It is for this reason, among others, that I have rejected the model of the original and the image as a satisfactory basis for explaining Platonic Ideas. Despite Plato's imagery, there is nothing visual about the apprehension of a Platonic Idea. The Idea of the cow is not a perfect portrait of what it is to be a cow, nor is it a perfect cow whose portrait we attempt to paint in the presence of actual cows.

What happens instead is that when we identify an actual cow, we realize (= "recollect") that the unity of this cow underlies the changing perceptual qualities in such a way that they do not prevent us from assigning the perceived cow to a definite kind. But unity can only be "seen" as this or that unity, and the precise identity of this particular unity is derived from the sameness of individual cows. In sum, I "see" the Idea of a cow when I see that this cow is the same as that one. But this is not to see a perfect cow standing over and apart from the perceived individual cows. Axiom 2 must therefore be modified to reject separation in the sense of distinguishing one world from another. The Idea of the cow is not an individual cow, but neither is it separate from individual cows.

There is one more objection to Axiom 2 that should be briefly considered. The Platonist has claimed that even though things are continuously changing, we must admit that it is in each case some definite thing that is undergoing change. Even the thesis that everything is turning into everything else depends upon the assumption that we can identify the turning of one thing into another. But what counts as the limit of change before something ceases to be of the same kind and becomes something else? We can agree that everything is what it is without knowing what it is, and so too we can know that something is of some kind or another even though we know very little about the nature of that kind. But in this case, it might be asked, how can we classify or identify anything at all?

The difficulty can be mitigated by the use of a previous argument. It is items of genesis that change, not Ideas. If the boundary between two kinds (or species) is impossible to determine because our sensory powers are inadequate to measure it, this means only that we will fail to notice the change in a given instance from one kind to another. But it does not mean that one kind will shift into another kind. The kind "Dinosaur" at some moment ceases to be instantiated; it is not transformed into the kind "reptile" or "bird."

The first two axioms of Platonism, then, may be summarized as follows. To be is to be of a certain kind, and the kind in question is not the same as the individuals *of* that kind. "Idea" is the word that Plato uses to distinguish the kind from its instances. The instances undergo change, which is to say that they come into being and pass away, but the kinds or Ideas do not. In this sense, we can say that the Ideas are eternal. This brings me to the third and last axiom. I note in passing that this axiom may more properly be thought of as a corollary to the second, but it is sufficiently important that I prefer to give it separate status. The axiom holds that the changing character of the instances of the domain of genesis makes it impossible for there to be genuine, that is to say precise and everlasting knowledge of them. But such knowledge is presumably possible of the Idea, and indeed, when we believe that we have obtained genuine knowledge of the instance, that knowledge is actually of the Idea.

But this knowledge has a very restricted nature. For example, as I have emphasized throughout, we can know that this is the same as that. And in those cases in which we are not sure whether this is the same as or other than that, we know that one or the other alternative is true, or in the worst case that we are in the presence of some third thing which is neither this nor that, but a thing of some other kind. What we do not know, or to be more cautious, what Plato never explains, is precisely what it is to be a cow. In other words, speaking very generally, there are two kinds of knowledge. One is of logical properties and the other is of what Kant calls "real predicates." The logical properties are the same in all cases. But the real predicates differ from thing to thing; hence, they must differ from Idea to Idea. The ontological properties of Ideas are presumably all the same in the case of each and every Idea. But what it is to be a cow is self-evidently different from what it is to be a horse, and this must be exhibited in the difference between the Idea of the cow and that of the horse.

If we were to ask Socrates "what is it to be a cow?" he might first refer to the logical predicates of the Idea of the cow but not to its real predicates. For example, he might say that to be a cow is to participate in sameness and otherness. But the same answer applies in the case of dogs or horses. What we are presently investigating is the question of what it is to be this particular kind of thing that we identify as a cow. One of the peculiarities of Platonism is that logical predicates of Ideas are much easier to identify than real predicates. In fact, although I have been using the language of predication here for the sake of convenience, it must now be abandoned, because the difference between subjects and predicates does not apply to Platonic Ideas. I can say that this cow is brown, but not that the Idea of the cow is brown. And this is of course true for every property of the cow. Please note that this is not true simply of accidental properties. Assuming that I knew the necessary and sufficient conditions for being a cow, I could still not apply these to the Idea of the cow, for if I could, it would then become a cow. This small point is of crucial importance. It is why we cannot assign what I will call "phenomenological" properties to Platonic Ideas.

So far as I can see, no Platonist has ever told us what it is to be a particular kind of thing, cow or otherwise, simply by reference to an Idea, even though the point of the Idea is in each case to exhibit what it is to be this or that thing. This holds even if we employ contemporary biological concepts and say for example that the DNA of the existing cow exhibits what it is to be a cow. It may very well, but Ideas do not possess DNA. Furthermore, if we identify the Idea of a natural kind with its DNA, the same distinction arises that we met previously: namely, the distinction between what it is to be DNA in general (=what it is to be an Idea) and what it is to be this particular DNA, namely, that of the cow (=the Idea of the cow). In order to discover the DNA of the cow, we analyze cows. We cannot derive any assistance in this task from the Idea-DNA because we have no information about its inner structure until we have discerned it in real cows.

So much for the sketch of what I have called the three axioms of Platonism understood as the doctrine of Ideas. This slightly cumbersome wording is necessary because one might reject the traditional or canonical conception of the doctrine of Ideas and still be a Platonist. For example, I myself accept the relevance of Platonic Ideas of logical entities and structures, but I am extremely dubious about the extension of the doctrine to other kinds of beings, such as cows and horses, not to mention justice and beauty, which time does not permit me to investigate more closely. My own explanation, or rather sketch of an explanation, of the Idea as the unity of some manifold clearly rests upon the rejection of the thesis of the separate and perfect original of which empirical instances are copies.[1]

Still, it is not quite impossible to extend the doctrine to cover empirical particulars. As I have tried to show, one could argue that there is a difference between knowledge of the formal structure of empirical particulars and knowledge of the necessary existence of Ideas. To know what it is to be something or another is not the same as to know that there exists a Platonic Idea that corresponds to what it is to be something or another. This line of argument seems to be in accord with Socrates' claim in the *Phaedo* that the Ideas are the most stable hypothesis. The hypothesis takes into account the fact that identifiable individuals exist, and that they possess formal properties that preserve identity despite the continuous change of the domain of genesis. The claim is then that formal structure is necessary if there is to be a world at all. It is, however, the structure of *this* world or domain and does not constitute another world or domain. As to the fact that Ideas differ with respect to the kinds of natural things such as cows, horses, and so on, the response is as follows. Ideas are under the same necessity as things to be this particular entity and none other. To be an Idea at all is to be the identifying structure of some kind. And kinds are identifiable only through difference. The simple explanation for why the Idea of the cow differs from the Idea of the horse is that cows differ from horses.

The Platonist response on this point also makes room for the obvious diversity in the kinds of Ideas that are discussed in the dialogues, ranging from ultimate ontological properties such as

1 [Ed.: For a highly speculative and in many ways quite different attempt to make sense of the Ideas, see Stanley Rosen, "Ideas," *Review of Metaphysics*, 16 (1963): 407–441. In that essay, Rosen relates the doctrine of Ideas to Plato's mathematical thought. As such, the idea is thought of in terms of the Monad (sameness or unity) and Dyad (otherness, or multiplicity). The Idea cannot be either of these by itself, of course. It is rather the triadic structure in which sameness and otherness are related in order to one another in such a way as to make possible the kind of determinacy necessary for Ideas to be the structure of the intelligibility of the entities of experience.]

same and other to Ideas of separate substances like cows and horses. It also replies to the objection that we study cows, not the Idea of the cow, in attempting to determine what it is to be a cow. The reply is that it is precisely the Idea that we are studying in this case, which Idea is not separate from the cow but is rather its intelligibility. It is obvious that in order to take this line of defense, one must give up all talk of complete separation of the Ideas, and so too the explanatory paradigm of original and image. In my opinion, this is a net gain for Platonism, not a loss.

We also eliminate an ambiguity in traditional Platonism to which I have not yet referred explicitly: the ambiguity of the relation between "Idea" and "kind." This is evident in the discussion of the one over many, in which we were said to gather together a collection of individuals of the same kind, while asserting that the particular kind in each case is the Idea of all individuals of that kind. If the Idea is the same as the kind, then we see it at once in the perceptual identification of any individual whatsoever as this thing here of such-and-such a kind. It is the sight of the Idea that allows us from the very outset to classify items correctly as of this rather than that kind. Therefore the study of Ideas is precisely the study of perceptible entities, and not of separate Ideas which are reflected in the empirical shape or nature of their instances. If Ideas were such separate entities, then on the hypothesis of the one over many, we would first see the reflections or images of Ideas in the looks or kinds of empirical objects, because this is precisely how we discover Ideas. We do not first identify empirical formal properties, which we call "copies" or "images" of the original, and then check these images against our separate perception of a separate Idea. The step from the kind to the Idea is entirely superfluous, not because there are no Ideas but because the Idea is the kind.

In sum: the best defense of Platonism is to reject all talk of separated Ideas. But we need not and should not reject the doctrine of recollection. I am of course not referring to its mythical formulation in conjunction with the doctrine of reincarnation, but to the empirically evident fact that we cannot know something of which we have no pre-awareness of any kind. When I encounter a strange object, the first thing I do (apart from experiencing fear, wonder, or some other emotion) is to attempt to classify it on the basis of my existing experience of kinds. This step is motivated, not by complete ignorance of the strange object, but rather by the recognition that it is strange, or in other words that it constitutes a new kind of being. This recognition in turn arises from the attempt to assimilate the strange object as closely as possible to one or a few already known kinds. We say: "X looks like a such-and-such in this way, but not in other ways." And so, step by step, we enact the process of division and collection in accord with kinds, moving outward from what is partly familiar toward those aspects of the strange object are perceived but not recognized. This outward motion is at each step made possible by the already existing structure of experience. Otherwise put, we are so consti-tuted by nature as to assume that whatever we encounter, no mat-ter how strange, can be classified as an instance of some kind or another.

In sum: we do not discover the Idea by an inference from our identification of the members of a determinate collection. On the contrary, in order to discover the individual element, and thus the entire multiplicity, we must first discover the Idea. What has to be emphasized is that we discover the Idea in the very act by which we establish the fact that this individual element is the same as that one. We don't move back and forth between two different worlds, but rather between two different dimensions of one and the same world. That we do not at the same time – or perhaps ever – understand that it is an Idea that we have discovered, is irrele-vant. As to the poetical accounts of the ascent of the cognitive soul to a hyperuranian *topos* of separate and perfect beings, we should, I believe, take this as Plato's way of emphasizing the marvelous nature of the intelligibility of this world, not of some other. In so doing, he also cautions us against the obstacles that stand in the path of retrospective analysis of the immediacy of intelligibility.

It should also be noticed that the present line of interpretation rejects Heidegger's account of Platonist *parousia*. In order to grasp the correct multiplicity, we must first see the Idea. But we see the Idea by recognizing each item in the multiplicity as of *the same kind*. That is, the Idea becomes visible not in itself, or as standing apart from all of its particular instances, but on the contrary as present within its instances. It is the particular element in the multiplicity that is of the same kind as each of the other elements. The expression "of the same kind" does not apply to the Idea but to the elements. One may object that when we ask "which kind is that?" we are referring to the Idea or one over many rather than to the many. My point, however, is that we cannot make this reference except by pointing to the elements of that kind. Nobody points to an Idea apart from elements of any kind. In sum, the Idea cannot be seen apart from its instances, and this constitutes a limitation on metaphysical presence, or what Heidegger calls *parousia* or *Anwesenheit*. What I referred to above as the immediacy of intelligibility is the full presence of the conditions that not only allow us to acquire knowledge of beings but that also restrict our capacity to analyze them. We can describe this immediacy in the excellent Heideggerian expression of the openness of the horizon. To know that the horizon is open is not the same as to try to analyze its structure. And besides, every step of analytical or calculative thinking is grounded in a prior awareness that cannot be reduced to elements of analysis.

Cumbersome though my analysis of the Ideas may be, the views that I recommend are in my opinion compatible with the actual ambiance of the Platonic corpus. I refer to the pervasive representation of philosophy as originating in ordinary experience. We have recourse to analytical and speculative reason in our effort to account for the coherence or immediacy of intelligibility, and so too of the immediacy of limitations on intelligibility. In a slightly paradoxical formulation, the limitations of intelligibility are also intelligible. In this sense, ordinary experience governs and prepares us for the pursuit of Platonic Ideas. Whether or not we can say with precision what it is to be something or another, the question never arises except as addressed to a being that has already been identified as a something or other. The famous

Heideggerian question of Being is itself a consequence of our analysis of the conditions for the existence of beings. But Heidegger deviates from Plato at this point. In the sense that Heidegger gives to the expression "Being," the Socratic question "*What is x?*"cannot be posed because Being is not a one *over* many. It is famously no "thing" at all, and hence not a definite one *among* many. Heideggerian Being is not a *what*. But this does not alter the fact that we are said to become aware of Being by the very process in which we see that it cannot be a one over many or definite entity.

This point leads to one more way in which to put the argument against separate Ideas. If Ideas were entirely separate from their instances, it would be difficult if not impossible to explain how one Idea differs from another. For example, in the Heideggerian exposition of the Being-process, that process of manifestation is the same everywhere, even though the manifested beings obviously differ, each from the others. But we cannot infer the properties of Being from our study of beings, because the very properties that make this being different from that one cannot be attributed to Being. In fact, Being has no properties at all, since each property is a determination, or a seeing of something *as* something, i.e., as something other than itself. If I may so put it, Heidegger suffers from a version of the *chôrismos* problem.

The immediate inference from the previous reflection is that there are no Ideas in general. Being is for Plato, of course, not general, but one of the "greatest genera," which is to say that it is not sameness, otherness, rest, or change. Ideas possess the same definiteness of identity as is to be found in generated particulars, albeit this definiteness is presumably unqualified and so permanent. The fact that there are many cows does not mean that there are many Ideas of the cow. On the contrary, the Idea of the cow is the perfect paradigm of what it is to be a cow and not another thing. To say that there is a second Idea of the cow is to say that cows have two identities, two distinct sets of conditions that make them cows. Let us say that this leads to the "third cow" regression.

Let me emphasize that we arrive at a vision of the identity of a cow, not by its independent manifestation antecedent to our experience with ordinary cows, but by a critical analysis of how it is possible for there to be anything at all, and why it is necessary that, if there is to be anything at all, it must be something of such-and-such a kind. I do not identify cows by glancing at the Idea of the cow; on the contrary, I am led to the Idea of the cow as what Socrates calls in the *Phaedo* the steadiest or most secure hypothesis about why I am able to identify cows. But this is perhaps stated too weakly. It is not a hypothesis but the first operation of cognition to see that each particular is not only the same as itself and other than every other, but also, that this individual is of the same kind as that one. Still more explicitly, we cannot help seeing the Idea, which is not just a (separate) kind, but the very kind of the individual we apprehend.

In sum, if genuine knowledge of the cow is actually knowledge of the Idea of the cow, it is nevertheless true that we arrive at knowledge of the Idea, if at all, then only through knowledge of the cow. The defining predicates of the cow are not elements in the Idea of the cow. We do not discover these predicates by turning away from the empirical cow in order to analyze the Idea. The study of Ideas is something quite different from the study of the properties of instances of Ideas. The question "what is it to be an Idea?" is quite different from the question "what is it to be a cow?" In what sense, then, can "knowing what it is to be a cow" be knowledge of the Idea of the cow?

In my opinion, the best answer to this question is as follows. In order for there to be things of any kind, there must be Ideas. But an Idea is not an original of which things are copies. Instead, it is the identity of a particular kind. Since things come in kinds, it follows that the Idea itself is of a particular kind. There are no Ideas in general. But there are general properties that belong to every particular Idea. This seems to entail that the eidetic properties of an Idea differ from the particular properties that make it an Idea of a particular collection of individuals. It is immediately obvious that what is peculiar to the identity of cows cannot also be peculiar to the identity of horses. At this point, I think it is necessary to deviate sharply from the traditional Platonist doctrine. We have to distinguish between the ontological properties of Ideas and the ontic properties of things. This formulation is in part Heideggerian, but Heidegger, of course, does not attribute ontological properties to Ideas. And as I have emphasized, "Idea" in my sense is not an original to be imitated, but the exhibition of the identity of a kind. We determine the kind by observing the particular things, and in order to give prominence to the difference between the kind and things of that kind, we hypostatize the kind and call it an Idea. It is at this point that the problems associated with separation emerge, and Platonism becomes an unintelligible or incoherent doctrine.

The point that I have been trying to make for the last several minutes is that there is a difference between being an instance of some kind or other, and being an instance of this particular kind. Both conditions, the general and the particular, characterize instances and are visible only within them, although once having reflected upon them, we can consider them apart from the instance by a process of abstraction. Let us refer to the study of kinds as ontology. There is, however, no general name for the study of particular kinds. It is not a part of ontology to study the nature of horses; this study belongs to some branch of zoology. Since kinds are kinds of individuals, they will be individual kinds. The kind "horse" is not the same as the kind "cow." But the two kinds will have properties in common that stem from their both being kinds. These properties will not explain what it is to be a horse or a cow, but only what it is to be an Idea. Finally, we see the kind (or "Idea") simultaneously with the apprehension of its instance as of such-and-such a kind. But to see this is not to see, either immediately or indirectly, what it is to be a horse. That, to repeat, must be discovered empirically.

It will certainly be objected by the orthodox Platonist that my modification of the doctrine of Ideas has led to their abolition. And there is a sense in which this is true, as is obvious from my rejection of separate Ideas. In particular, I have rejected the notion of an Idea as the paradigmatic original of a family of individuals that provide us with blurred copies of the original. Finally, it could be objected that I have accepted Ideas in the purely formal or logical sense of properties like identity, difference, and sameness, properties which at best account for the common structure of every particular Idea, whereas I have left unexplained, or relegated to the empirical or ontic level, what it is to be a cow, a horse, and so on. But this objection would be based upon a misunderstanding. My thesis is certainly not that there are only Ideas in general, but no Ideas in particular. On the contrary, every Idea is a particular Idea. What I insist upon is that the particularity of the Idea cannot be accounted for on the basis of the general properties of Ideas. How could one derive the eidetic look of the cow from identity, difference, and sameness (to mention only these)?

But this explanation seems only to leave the objection intact. For how can we derive the eidetic properties of what it is to be a cow from the empirical properties such as "four footed," "chews a cud," "yields milk," and so on? The answer is that we cannot, because *there are no purely eidetic properties of what it is to be a cow.* There are instead empirical properties that are subject to change. What does not change is the fact that we can perceive and study the empirical cow because of its adherence to the ontological properties of the structure of intelligibility that Plato regularly speaks of as "Ideas." It is this structure that regulates change and makes changing things intelligible.

What it means to be a cow may therefore change, but what will not change is our ability to identify what we mean by "being a cow." In Plato's mythical language, the Good casts its light on the Ideas and makes them visible. The Idea of the cow, taken as a particular Idea, stands for the intelligibility of the empirical cow, that is, for our ability to understand what it is to be a cow by studying cows. We can do this, not because there is a supreme or fully present cow standing above all real cows, at which we are actually looking for knowledge of cows in general, but because the ontological structure of intelligibility necessarily manifests itself as this or that kind of thing.

What does it mean, then, to claim, as does orthodox Platonism, that whereas we take ourselves to be looking at empirical entities in the pursuit of knowledge, what we are actually looking at is the Idea or Ideas of these empirical entities? The only sense I can attribute to this claim is that the Idea of the cow is in fact present in each cow, and is not different from the kind of thing that cows are. It is therefore wrong to say that, in grasping the necessary and sufficient properties of cowhood, we are studying the Idea of the cow, as though we were reading a map or duplicating a painting of something that is independent of, and even transcends, what it is to be a cow. Our empirical knowledge of the nature of the cow may very well be incomplete at any time, but it is the intelligible nature of the kind of things cows are that makes it possible for empirical knowledge to be accumulated in the first place. And we discover this possibility by engaging in the process of acquiring knowledge, not by gazing at Ideas.

This conclusion, if it obtains, does not bring with it the dissolution of intelligibility. On the contrary, it sticks close to the common-sense view that intelligibility is fully ensconced within things, and that this follows from the fact that to be is to be something of such-and-such a kind, a way of putting the point that is, I believe, common to Plato and Aristotle. I cannot explain why there is something rather than nothing, or for that matter why there is consciousness of intelligibility. But there is nothing puzzling about the denial that things are mere generalities, or that they lack a definite identity. We say that the cow changes, and not, in imitation of Heidegger, that change changes.

What then are we to say about the issue of production? My own view is that we produce, or share in the production of, a good many things, including the instances of perceptual experience. We also produce the calculative reasoning by which the formal properties of experience are rendered more fully intelligible. But we cannot produce the formal properties themselves. For example, our neurophysiology, together with the laws of optics, produces the sensory individual known in everyday life as a cow. But it does not produce the fact that to be is to be something of such-and-such a kind. Nor does it produce the fact that to be knowable as a cow, that is, as the object of empirical study, the perceptual elements of the cow must obey the laws of identity, difference, and sameness.

It is now time to bring these lectures to a close. Let me remind you that there are no solutions to genuine philosophical problems. With respect to metaphysical production, the safest hypothesis is in my view the one that is presented to us by everyday life. No one can seriously deny the immediate inference from the acts of identification (and so too of misidentification), to the fact of intelligibility. What Heidegger calls "metaphysics" is the attempt to account for the fact of intelligibility as the production of its foundations or pre-conditions. I have tried to persuade you that no such doctrine is to be found in Plato. The doctrine that we produce the conditions of order cannot even be stated coherently, let alone adequately defended. The most we could do is to affirm the Kantian hypothesis that the conditions of order are constituted by the spontaneity of thinking. On this hypothesis, it would be more accurate to say that we are ourselves produced by the activity of cognition than that we produce it. The rules of order must be obeyed if we are to exist.

I have time to make one last extended remark about the issue of metaphysical production. As the argument has developed, there are two serious possibilities with respect to answers to the question "where are forms located?" I have been more or less calling these the Platonist and the Kantian alternatives. On the Platonist alternative, the forms are in some hyperuranian *topos*. Somewhat less metaphorically, they exist outside the processes of mentation and are discovered by our perceptual and cognitive activity. On the Kantian alternative, the forms are what I will call "potencies" of thinking itself. They are not simply discovered, because our thinking activates them. But neither are they simply produced, because they express universal conditions that all creatures like ourselves must obey, and this would be true even if we produced the forms. That is, production itself is rule-bound. There is no thinking outside or beyond the compass of the transcendental concepts and rules by which the latter are constituted. They constitute themselves spontaneously as thinking occurs.

In my view, Heidegger's central obsession with the covering over of Being by beings is as applicable to Kant as it is to Plato. In both cases, the beings (*ta onta*) are constituted by the combined activity of sense perception and predicates available only to pure reason, whether we call these Ideas or concepts. In other words, Kant accepts the Platonist-Aristotelian thesis that to be is to be something definite and of such and such a kind. In neither case does one find any mention of a Being (*Sein*) that is not this or that entity of such and such a kind. The closest one comes to this is the reference to *epekeina tês ousias* in the *Republic*, but this refers to the Idea of the Good, and so is once more given a determinate, if difficult to analyze, identity. For Kant, of course, being is not a real predicate. It does not enter into the structure of an object in such a way as to differentiate one kind of object from another. Stated as simply as possible, for Kant, to be is to have a position within the world that is accessible to the scientific pursuit of knowledge. No one being differs from any other in the way that cows differ from horses, and every being in the world is the same as every other being in the sense that all have position. Differences of position can themselves be identified only by the differences in the objects that occupy them, but these latter differences, as I have just noted, are furnished by the object-predicates in each case.

This brief inspection of Kant was intended merely to bring out the underlying similarity between Plato and Kant, not to mention Aristotle, on the central question of metaphysical production. Similarity is of course not identity. But the differences are not so great as to obliterate the similarity.

Selected Bibliography

Bernasconi, Robert. "Heidegger's Destruction of *Phronêsis.*" *Southern Journal of Philosophy*, 28 (Supplement): 127–47.

Boutot, Alain. *Heidegger et Platon: Le Probleme du Nihilisme*. Paris: Presse Universitaires de France, 1987.

Brague, Remi. "Radical Modernity and the Roots of Ancient Thought." *The Independent Journal of Philosophy*, vol. 4 (1983): 63–74.

Brogan, Walter J. "A Response to Robert Bernasconi's 'Heidegger's Destruction of *Phronêsis.*'" *Southern Journal of Philosophy*, 28:S149–53.

Caputo, John D. *Demythologizing Heidegger*. Bloomington, Ind.: Indiana University Press, 1993.

Dahlstrom, Daniel O. *Heidegger's Concept of Truth*. Cambridge: Cambridge University Press, 2001.

Dostal, Robert J. "Beyond Being: Heidegger's Plato." *Journal of the History of Philosophy*, 23 (1):71–98.

Figal, Günter. "Refraining from Dialectic: Heidegger's Interpretation of Plato in the *Sophist* Lecture," in

Interrogating the Tradition: Hermeneutics and the History of Philosophy, ed. C.E. Scott and John Sallis. Albany: SUNY Press, 2000: 95–109.

Fried, Gregory. "Back to the Cave: A Platonic Rejoinder to Heideggerian Post-Modernism." In *Heidegger and the Greeks: Interpretative Essays*, edited by Drew Hyland, John P. Manoussakis. Bloomington, Ind.: Indiana University Press, 2006: 157–176.

Gadamer, Hans-Georg. *Dialogue and Dialectic: Eight Hermeneutical Studies on Plato*. Translated by P. Christopher Smith. New Haven: Yale University Press, 1980.

_____. "Die Griechen," in *Heideggers Wege: Studien zum Spätwerk* (Tuebingen: Mohr, 1983).

Galston, William A. – "Heidegger's Plato: A Critique of *Plato's Doctrine of Truth*." *Philosophical Forum* 13 (1982): 371–384.

Partenie, Catalin and Rockmore, Tom, eds. *Heidegger and Plato: Toward Dialogue*. Evanston, Ill.: Northwestern University Press, 2005.

Hyland, Drew and Manoussakis, John P., eds. *Finitude and Transcendence in the Platonic Dialgoues*. Albany: SUNY Press, 1995.

_____. *Heidegger and the Greeks. Interpretative Essays*. Bloomington, Ind.: Indiana University Press, 2006.

Kisiel, Theodore. *The Genesis of Heidegger's Being and Time*. Berkeley: University of California Press, 1993.

Krüger, Gerhard. *Einsicht und Leidenschaft. Das Wesen des*

platonischen Denkens. Frankfurt am Main: Vittorio Klosterman, 1992.

Pippin, Robert. *Modernity as Philosophical Problem: On the Dissatisfactions of European High Culture*. Cambridge, Mass: Basil Blackwell, 1991.

Richardson, William J. *Heidegger: Through Phenomenology to Thought*. The Hague: Martinus Nijhoff, 1967.

Rojcewicz, Richard. "Platonic Love: Dasein's Urge toward Being." *Research in Phenomenology* 27:103–120.

Rosen, Stanley. *The Question of Being: A Reversal of Heidegger*. South Bend, Ind.: St. Augustine's Press, 2002.

Sallis, John. *Being and Logos: Reading the Platonic Dialogues*. Bloomington, Ind.: Indiana University Press, 1996.

Zuckert, Catherine H. *Postmodern Platos*. Chicago: University of Chicago Press, 1996.

References and Abbreviations

Unless noted otherwise below, references to Heidegger's works will be to the German text in the *Gesamtausgabe*, published by Klostermann (Frankfurt a.M.), 1975. For ease of reference, the German pagination will be followed by the page number of the relevant English translation, where this was available. When preparing this manuscript, the editor did not have available GA, 5 (*Holzwege*) containing the essays, "Die Zeit des Weltbildes" and "Nietzsches Wort 'Gott ist tot'." Accordingly, references to these essays are to William Lovitt's English translation. Abbreviations of Platonic and Aristotelian titles follow those in Liddell, Scott, and Jones Lexicon.

AWP		"Age of the World Picture", in *The Question Concerning Technology and Other Essays*, trans. William Lovitt (New York: Harper and Row, 1977), 115–154.
EM	*Einführung in die Metaphysik*, GA 40.	*Introduction to Metaphysics*, trans. Gregory Fried and Richard Polt (New Haven: Yale Nota Bene, 2000).

EP "Das Ende der Philosophie
und die Aufgabe des
Denkens", in *Zur Sache des
Denkens*, GA, 14.

FNT "Die Frage nach der
Technik", in *Vorträge und
Aufsätze*, GA, 7.

"The Question Concerning
Technology", in *The
Question Concerning
Technology and Other
Essays*, trans. by William
Lovitt (New York: Harper
and Row, 1977), 3–35.

GBM *Die Grundbegriffe der
Metaphysik*, GA 29/30.

*The Basic Concepts of
Metaphysics*, trans. William
McNeill and Nicholas
Walker (Bloomington, Ind:
Indiana University Press,
1995).

GPP *Die Grundprobleme der
Phänomenologie*, GA 24.

*Basic Problems of
Phenomenology*, trans.
Albert Hofstadter
(Bloomington, Ind.: Indiana
University Press, 1982).

HHA *Hölderlins Hymne
"Andenken"*, GA 52.

HB "Brief über den
Humanismus", in
Wegmarken, 2nd ed.
(Frankfurt a.M.: 1978).

"Letter on 'Humanism'", in
Pathmarks, ed. William
McNeill (Cambridge:
Cambridge University Press,
1998), 239–276.

K	"Die Kehre", in *Identität und Differenz*, GA 11.	"The Turning", in *The Question Concerning Technology and Other Essays*, trans. by William Lovitt (New York, Harper and Row, 1977), 36–49.
MAL	*Metaphysische Anfangsgründe der Logik im Ausgang von Leibniz*, GA 26.	*The Metaphysical Foundations of Logic*, trans. Michael Heim (Bloomington: Indiana University Press, 1984).
N	*Nietzsche I und II* (Pfullingen, Germany: Neske Verlag, 1961).	*Nietzsche*, vols. 1 and 2, trans. David Farrell Krell (New York: Harper Collins, 1991). *Nietzsche*, vols. 3 and 4, trans. David Farrell Krell (New York: Harper Collins, 1991).
NW		"The Word of Nietzsche: 'God is Dead'", in *The Question Concerning Technology and Other Essays*, trans. by William Lovitt (New York: Harper and Row, 1977), 53–112.
P	*Parmenides*, in GA 54.	*Parmenides*, trans. André Schuwer and Richard Rojcewicz (Bloomington, Ind.: Indiana University Press, 1992).

PLW   "Platons Lehre von der Wahrheit", in *Wegmarken* (Frankfurt a.M.: Vittorio Klostermann, 1978), 201–236.   "Plato's Doctrine of Truth," in *Pathmarks*, ed. William McNeill (Cambridge: Cambridge University Press, 1998), 155–182.

PS   *Platon: Sophistes*, GA 19.   *Plato's Sophist*, trans. Richard Rojcewicz and Andre Schuwer (Bloomington, Ind: Indiana University Press, 1997).

SZ   *Sein und Zeit*, 15th ed. (Tübingen: Niemeyer Verlag, 1984).   *Being and Time*, trans. John Macquarrie and Edward Robinson (San Francisco: Harper and Row, 1962).

WBP   *Vom Wesen und Begriff der* φύσις: Aristotels, Physik B, 1 (1939), in *Wegmarken*, 2nd ed. (Frankfurt a.M.: 1978), 237–299.   "On the Essence and Concept of φύσις in Aristotle's Physics B, 1 (1939), in *Pathmarks*, ed. William McNeill (Cambridge: Cambridge University Press, 1998), 183–230.

WdW   *Vom Wesen der Wahrheit* GA 34.   *The Essence of Truth*, trans. Ted Sadler (London: Continuum, 2002).

WM   "Was ist Metaphysik?" in *Wegmarken*, 2nd ed. (Frankfurt a.M.: 1978), 103–122.   "What is Metaphysics?" in *Pathmarks*, ed. William McNeill (Cambridge: Cambridge University Press, 1998), 82–96.

WMF   *Vom Wesen der Menschlichen Freiheit: Einleitung in die Philosophie*, GA 31.

On the Essence of Human Freedom: An Introduction to Philosophy, trans. Ted Sadler (London: Continuum, 2002).

Index